Mixtape Memories Vol. 1

First Edition
ISBN: 979-8-9991023-0-0
Cover design by Sally Silva
Back cover image courtesy of Olya Bik Photography

Independently Published
www.michellewolfe.me | info@michellewolfe.me

Printed in the United States of America

To my children—your light, your laughter, and your limitless curiosity inspire me every day. You are the greatest melody in my life, the song that never fades, the harmony that carries me forward. I'm so proud to be your Mom.

To the ones who evoked such depth of emotion within me that I could write this—I appreciate you.

And to the girl I used to be and the woman I have become—for the strength to feel, the courage to heal, and the willingness to turn pain into something beautiful. This book is proof that every emotion has a place, every story matters, and every heartache can become a song.

Table of Contents

Foreword

Preface

Part 1: The Journey Within
Exploring self-discovery, healing, and personal growth.

- *Vica Versa* – Pastor Troy (50)
  Written by Kimberly Belk
  A reflective journey of challenging rigid definitions of good and evil, inspired by duality and the nuanced exploration of morality.

- *Would?* – Alice in Chains (57)
  Written by Matthew Solomon
  Navigating heartbreak and adversity through music.

- *Help Me to Feel Again* – Judah and the Lion (60)
  Written by Becca Zelner
  Healing through grief and rediscovering emotional connection.

Part 2: Growth, Resilience, & The Bonds That Shape Us
Relationships, connection, love, and longing.

- *Wish You Were Here* – Incubus (66)
  Written by Becca Zelner
  Longing for connection with both the absent and distant.

- *I'll Stand By You* – The Pretenders (71)
  Written by Joie Costa
  Redefining loyalty and finding strength in self-devotion.

- *Forever Young* – Rod Stewart (77)
  Written by Michelle Wolfe
  A nostalgic tribute to childhood, parenthood, and the timeless hope of staying young at heart.

- *Nothing Compares 2 U* – Sinead O'Connor (82)
  Written by Melissa Rymer
  Navigating love, loss, and the evolution of self.

- ***Your Ex-Lover is Dead*** – Stars (86)
  Written by Jeremy Nigli
  Letting go of relationships and finding resilience.

- ***November Rain*** – Guns N' Roses (97)
  Written by Michelle Wolfe
  Transforming heartbreak into empowerment and self-love.

- ***You Get What You Give*** – New Radicals (104)
  Written by Jennifer Eggerts
  A journey of recovery and self-discovery, inspired by the enduring hope of a song that became a lifeline through struggles with addiction and trauma.

- ***Time After Time*** – Cyndi Lauper (111)
  Written by Michelle Wolfe
  A love that transcends distance, a song that refuses to be ignored, and the quiet knowing that some connections always find their way back.

- ***With You I'm Born Again*** – Billy Preston & Syreeta Wright (116)
  Written by Mariyam Hasham
  Exploring compassion and transformation through love and music.

- ***Do You Wanna Make Love*** – Peter McCann (121)
  Written by Louis Cinquino
  Humorous lessons in vulnerability and romantic fantasies.

- ***Down Bad*** – Taylor Swift (129)
  Written by Michelle Wolfe
  Confronting attachment wounds and embracing self-growth.

Part 3: The Soundtrack of Transformation

The transformative and healing power of music.

- *The Wall* – Pink Floyd (135)
  Written by Kian Eder
  Music as a gateway to healing and dismantling emotional barriers.

- *I Saw Her Standing There* – The Beatles (142)
  Written by Denise VanBriggle
  The precious moments wrapped up in a song that transports you to another time.

- *Unspoken* – The Soil (146)
  Written by Ruthie Lerato
  Reconnecting with ancestral roots through lyricless music.

- *The Sign* – Nujabes (156)
  Written by Brett Ward
  Finding awareness and purpose amidst societal challenges.

- *Rocky Mountain High* – John Denver (160)
  Written by Jeanne Edwards
  Nature and music as tools for renewal and introspection.

- *Happy* – Pharrel Williams (167)
  Written by Michelle Wolfe
  The science of music, movement, and joy—how a song can instantly shift mood and energy.

- *Beautiful Dawn* – The Wailin' Jennys (173)
  Written by Murshida VA
  Spiritual transformation and embracing collective liberation.

- *Maybe It's Just Me* – Butch Walker (187)
  Written by Scott Lester
  Exploring selflessness and resilience in love's aftermath.

- *Skylarkin'* – Mic Christopher (191)
  Written by Elizabeth Evelyn Bond
  Self-discovery, and the importance of remaining curious and authentic.

- *Times Like These* – Foo Fighters (197)
  Written by Michelle Wolfe
  A song of transition, reflection, and the choices that shape who we become.

Closing Reflections

- **Final Note: Writing the Soundtrack of Our Lives**

Acknowledgments

- Special thanks to the contributing authors, various artists, and everyone who collaborated to make this project possible.

Foreword

The Harmony of Healing: Music is Good for the Soul

Music has been woven into the fabric of human experience for millennia. From the rhythmic beats of ancient drums to the sweeping melodies of symphonies, music transcends culture, language, and time. It stirs something primal and universal within us, becoming a vehicle for emotions, memories, and even our very sense of identity.

It has always been more than sound; it's a heartbeat, a lifeline. Music moves through us, shaping the moments we live and the ones we never want to forget. It connects the isolated with the universal, helping us express the inexpressible and make sense of the chaos within. As a mental health professional, I have witnessed firsthand its transformative power and have even prescribed it as medicine. It has also been a tool for my clients to show me exactly how they feel on the inside. Music has this uncanny ability to say what we can't—or won't—and that's what makes it magic. The best part? It doesn't require an appointment, and it's always there when you need it.

The Emotional Resonance of Music

Music has a unique ability to affect our emotions. It reaches into places words cannot touch. Research in the fields of psychology and neuroscience has consistently demonstrated the profound impact it can have on mood. It can make you smile, cry, or dance with abandon, sometimes all in the same song. Neuroscience backs this up, showing that music stimulates the release of dopamine—the same neurotransmitter that lights us up when we're falling in love, eating chocolate, or laughing with friends. It's why the right song at the right time feels like it was made just for you.

Moreover, music has been shown to have a regulatory effect on the autonomic nervous system. For example, slow, calming music can decrease heart rate, lower blood pressure, and reduce levels of the stress hormone cortisol. On the other hand, upbeat, fast-paced music can increase arousal and energy levels. The capacity to modulate physiological states is just one reason why music is used in therapeutic settings like my clinic to help individuals manage anxiety, depression, stress, grief and more.

Music as a Bridge to Memory

Music plays a significant role in memory, helping us hold onto pieces of ourselves that we thought we'd lost. Even when memories fade, music endures. I've seen it unlock vivid recollections for individuals with Alzheimer's, connecting them to moments they thought were gone forever. The brain's connection to music is a wonder—activating emotion, memory, and movement all at once.

This phenomenon is supported by research in cognitive neuroscience which shows that music activates multiple areas of the brain, including regions involved in memory, emotion, and even motor control. One reason for this is that music is often linked to personal experiences, making it a potent trigger for autobiographical memories. A song from our youth might bring back vivid memories of a particular time, place, or person and how we felt in that moment. This is why you'll see people say that the songs that were popular when you were hitting puberty are likely going to be the ones that you're "stuck on" later.

As someone who came of age in the 1990's, artists like Enigma, Celine Dion, P!nk, New Kids on the Block and later Backstreet Boys, as well as various R&B and alternative/ grunge chart toppers are some of the first to get me going on any given day. I had my first kiss to "The Power of Love" (*Celine Dion*) and used to blare "Zombies" (*Cranberries*) whenever I was mad at my parents. When my brother died, the "Tarzan" (1999) soundtrack would make me cry because it was the last movie we saw together, but you'd find me listening to it on repeat just to feel him near me again.

Embracing the Healing Power of Music

Music isn't just entertainment. It's a truth-teller, a lifeline, a pulse that reminds us we're alive. It doesn't sugarcoat. It doesn't ask permission. It simply is. Music demands that we confront ourselves, feel deeply, and find our rhythm in a world that doesn't always make sense. It's a relentless testament pulsating through our humanity, raw and unapologetic.

And that's why when Michelle first told me about her passion project, I was jazzed (*every pun intended*). Music is the great equalizer, a universal drug that cuts across the bullshit, tearing down the walls we've built around ourselves. This project is everything music represents: connection, healing, and truth. Music doesn't care who you are, where you've been, or what you've lost—it meets you where you are. Each chapter of this anthology is a song brought to life, a testament to the way music shapes our lives and holds our stories. These authors have poured their hearts into these pages, inviting you to feel alongside them, to remember your own songs, your own moments.

Composers, musicians and artists would tell you it's not meant to be just a background to our lives but a vibrant, living entity that moves *through* us, animating our life force. I often tell clients to imagine they're living in their own music video and create from THAT space. "*How do you want to feel?*" I'll ask them. "*Because new stimuli, new feels.*"

So, I ask you dear one, what would be the soundtrack of YOUR life?

This isn't background noise we're talking about. This is the music that gets you out of bed in the morning, the melody that carried you through heartbreak, the beat that made you feel alive for the first time in years. Don't settle for sanitized silence. Feel it. Live it. Let it remind you that, despite everything, you're here—and that matters.

With love and solidarity for your journey,

Tamara Driskell
Psychotherapist & Coach

Preface

Mixtape Memories: The Songs of Your Life

Music is a universal language, a shared heartbeat that transcends time, space, and culture. It's the soundtrack to our lives, weaving its way into our most profound memories and shaping who we are. Songs don't just accompany our stories; they shape them, they *become* them, carrying the weight of our heartbreaks, our joy, and our quiet moments of self-discovery. *Mixtape Memories* was born out of this truth—the idea that behind every song lies a story, and behind every story is a human experience waiting to be shared.

This anthology is more than a collection of essays; it's a playlist of emotions, memories, and connections. Each chapter takes you on a journey, tethered to a specific song that resonated deeply with its author. These songs were not just background noise—they were catharses, lifelines, and moments of clarity during some of life's most pivotal and vulnerable experiences.

Through the lens of music, we've explored love, heartbreak, grief, self-discovery, and resilience. Some of us found solace in lyrics that seemed to articulate what we couldn't. Others found themselves transported to specific times and places, where a single note could evoke joy, longing, or bittersweet nostalgia. These stories invite you to reflect on your own mixtape of memories, to rediscover the songs that shaped you and the emotions they still hold.

The beauty of music lies in its ability to create connection— not just between artist and listener but between all of us. When we hear a song that speaks to us, we feel seen, understood, and less alone. *Mixtape Memories* aims to do the same, providing a space for shared humanity through stories tied to the universal power of song.

This book is for anyone who has ever pressed rewind to relive a feeling, who has danced alone in their kitchen to shake off a heartbreak, or who has found unexpected tears welling up as a song came on the radio. It's for anyone who has ever needed music to say what they couldn't, to hold them in their pain, or to lift them in their triumph.

Music, at its core, is about connection—to each other, to ourselves, and to the emotions we sometimes can't put into words. The authors of *Mixtape Memories* have shared their hearts with you, baring their truths and inviting you into their world. We hope these stories inspire you to reflect on your own, to revisit the songs that have carried you through life, and to see the beauty in the moments they represent.

This project would not have been possible without the incredible authors and collaborators who poured their hearts and souls into these pages. To the storytellers who relived their moments of vulnerability and courage to share them with the world: thank you for your honesty, your openness, and your trust. Your words breathe life into this collection and create a symphony of experiences that will resonate with readers for years to come.

To the collaborators, editors, and everyone who lent their expertise, energy, and passion to this project: thank you for your dedication and belief in what *Mixtape Memories* could be. Your support, insight, and encouragement transformed this dream into a reality.

And to the remarkable artists and musicians who crafted the songs that have shaped and inspired us—this book is as much a tribute to you as it is a reflection of our lives. Your creative genius and courage to share your art have left an indelible mark on the world. Through your music, you have given us the tools to feel deeply, to express what words alone cannot, and to connect with one another across time and space. Your songs have been our companions in solitude, our anthems in triumph, and our solace in heartbreak.

We hope that, should you or your loved ones read these pages, you'll see the profound impact your music has had on our lives. The stories within this book stand as a testament to the ways your art has helped us make sense of our worlds, heal our wounds, and celebrate our joys.

Together, we have created something beautifully meaningful—a book that bridges hearts and minds, reminding us all of the power of storytelling and the timeless magic of music.

So, press play, and let the music guide you.

Press Play on Your Experience

To fully immerse yourself in the stories and emotions of *Mixtape Memories*, we've curated a Spotify playlist featuring the songs that inspired these chapters. Each track carries the essence of the stories within these pages, and we invite you to listen along as you read.

Whether you're revisiting an old favorite or discovering something new, the playlist is your personal soundtrack to this journey.

You can find the playlist by scanning the QR code or by searching for *Mixtape Memories* on Spotify.

Mixtape Memories Spotify Playlist

Let the music bring the stories to life.

We've curated a special playlist to accompany the chapters in this collection—a sonic backdrop for your journey through memory, meaning, and emotion.

Search "Mixtape Memories" on Spotify or scan the barcode below to listen along as you read.

Scan here!

Disclaimer

This book is a deeply personal exploration of memory, meaning, and music. Some chapters include brief excerpts of song lyrics that have been transformative, cathartic, or significant to the author's lived experience.

These excerpts are included under the doctrine of fair use, specifically for the purposes of commentary, reflection, and transformative expression. The lyrics are limited in scope, used in a non-commercial, non-substitutive way, and always in direct connection to the author's lived experience.

All rights to the original lyrics and compositions remain with their respective copyright holders. With deep respect and gratitude, we honor the artists and songs that have shaped our stories and inspired the words within these pages.

All rights to the original lyrics and compositions remain fully with the respective copyright holders. The songs included are acknowledged with deep respect and gratitude for their influence and emotional resonance.

Mixtape Memories

The Songs of Your Life

Let the Music Play…
Let the Stories Begin…

Part 1: The Journey Within
Exploring self-discovery, healing, and personal growth.

"Through music, we may wander where we will in time, and find ourselves again." – Helen Thompson

Mixtape Memories

Author: Martha Truxton Heller

It's late in the day as I drive home.

"Yellow Ledbetter" filters in on the radio, carrying my mind back to moments long since gone. My thoughts return to those days back in high school when I would drive to nowhere just to clear my head. I glance in the rearview mirror and notice the storm rolling in behind me. The sky in that mirror is threateningly dark, yet the road home in front of me stretches out into a brilliant blue. The contrast is startling. As I watch, the sky behind grows ever darker with each minute that passes. The storm chases me as my thoughts keep tumbling backwards... looking behind; staring in the rearview. It feels like I'm often this way: stuck in a distant memory. Trying to get somewhere I can never return to.

For as long as I can remember, I have had this restlessness in my spirit that plays with my desperation for stability, and roots that sink deep. My past persistently interfering with my present. The two, forever at odds; forever struggling. Music, quite often, is what carries me backwards, keeping my eyes from watching the road ahead. That distracting rearview mirror. Music is so intricately entangled with significant moments in my life—it has imprinted so deeply into thoughts long-forgotten—that it has this unsettling way of taking me to a million different moments in my life without warning. Every song I hear beckons me along one path or another and soon I am lost down a rabbit hole of ruminations.

Music, for me, is saturated with memories.

I recall music playing on the 8-track in our old Peugeot as we would drive around on the red dirt roads back home in Nigeria. I was too young to remember the songs, but I do remember those clunky cartridges. When our old car finally had a tape deck, cassettes would play on repeat during our countless long car trips around the country. I remember Simon and Garfunkel, Chicago, Panam Percy Paul...

A few years later, Phil Collins played on the tape deck in our friends' yellow Toyota minivan as we rode to school, drawing pictures with our fingers in the condensation that clung to the windows. In the afternoons, my best friend and I would listen to the Beatles on a little Sony cassette player in my room; our soundtrack while we painted, or danced, or looked through teen magazines from America. On Saturdays we would bike that same little tape deck all the way out to Rayfield Lake on the outskirts of town. We spread towels out on the red dirt by the lake and listened to U2 while we sat and watched the red lake and talked about boys.

I have other memories of being alone, lying on the floor of my room and journaling for hours, the Cure thrumming in my ears...

I remember loud music playing in the cars of high school friends as we would drive around all the backroads at night and sing as loud as we could: Khaled, Guns N Roses, Jane's Addiction, Nirvana...

Some of my most difficult years were my late high school and early college years, when I often couldn't put words to how I was feeling or what I was going through as a third culture teenager. A lot of my old journals are littered with song lyrics; all the sentiments I hadn't been able to name but someone else was gifted enough to capture in words.

Music gave me a voice. It summoned the things deeply buried that I couldn't drag to the surface on my own.

Music brought out my anger, joy, despair, the ache of wanting... And I know it was the same for so many of my peers.

Music was one of the biggest ways we communicated with each other. We would listen together as we drove aimlessly at night, singing along loudly and happily, or sometimes staring quietly out the dark windows, letting our silence and the music fill the distance between us.

We took so many of those songs that spoke for us and compiled them onto cassette tapes for each other. Like a handwritten note, passed stealthily in a crowded classroom. We often didn't even know what we wanted to say, but we knew how the music made us feel. I still remember the thrill of snapping a newly received mixtape into my tape deck and, just lying on my bed staring at my splatter-painted walls, getting completely lost in it. I recall making some of those mixtapes. Sitting on the floor of my room, tape deck plugged in, unwrapping a blank cassette, finding just the right songs that evoked just the right feelings. The songs that communicated the things I either couldn't say or couldn't find the words for. The songs that took me places I wanted others to follow.

My friends and I made a lot of mixtapes for each other...I have stacks of them still. Each cover decorated with patterns or pictures cut out of magazine pages, every song title written by hand on the inner cover. Each compilation with a title that was creatively conjured and scrawled onto the spine of the outer case: "a spectrum of innocence," "memoirs," "music to take home to mom," "something good I have to give..."

One of my favorite mixtapes is titled "hero" and was given to me back in early high school by a close friend who had moved away. We were inseparable for most of our elementary years, and when her family moved to America after our 6th grade year, I was lost. I spent a lot of time isolated and alone after she left. But we kept in touch, and one day she mailed me a mixtape. It was a compilation of songs she wrote and sang herself, interspersed with songs she had played with her band "Daisyhead." It was a very restoring experience to listen to something she had created; a piece of her sent to me over oceans. Woven delicately through her lyrics was a message, revealing to me that she was a lesbian: a secret that (at that time) was really heavy for her. And I had been entrusted with it. I held it close.

"Bittersweet Memories" was given to me by my Australian sister. We grew up together in a little town called Jos in the middle of Nigeria. Her family lived just across the dirt road from our house, and we made an endless amount of memories together. Sleepovers, campouts in each other's back yards, riding bikes all over the compound where we lived, climbing guava trees and Flame trees, making necklaces out of the Plumeria that dropped in front of her house, swimming in the old tin-mining lake in Rayfield...but just as high school began, her family moved back to Australia and I lost my closest friend in the whole wide of the world. She made "Bittersweet Memories" for me just before she left. It had all of the songs we would listen to on repeat for hours and hours, in her room or mine.

Such beautiful memories, laced with the bitterness of goodbye. It was a precious compilation that I listened to on repeat for many years. As time rolled relentlessly forward, she sent me many other mixtapes, each a precious piece of herself. Each compilation was her, reaching across the distance between us and reminding me that she was still in my life. Still my sweet sister.

I received "group therapy" at a time in my later high school years when I was deeply struggling. I grappled daily with issues of identity, spirituality, strained friendships, depression, intense anxiety about everything...I often felt paralyzed under the weight, and it took a toll on me physically. Many nights I couldn't sleep at all. I would watch the clock, counting down the hours until daylight, and I found myself pulling away from many of my closest friends. However, just when I was in one of my darkest hours, one of them took the time to compile a tape of encouraging songs for me. Her gesture broke me open. It meant the world that she had seen my need and had extended her hands in friendship. It didn't remove my anxieties, but it was such a sweet balm for my very weary spirit. It really was a kind of therapy. It was a glimpse of hope.

These mixtapes of mine—these solid memories I can turn over in my hands—these snapshots of moments from long ago; my friends' handwriting, their creativity, the hours spent thinking of me and compiling songs…they undo me, at times. These memories undo me.

I guess that's why I often get trapped there. Trying to move beyond an immense amount of complicated memories— layered memories—and fight to be present feels so futile sometimes.

Some of these tapes I have listened to so often that I can hear the next song beginning before the current one ends…And isn't that how my anxious mind works? I anticipate what's coming before I sit fully with what I have in front of me. I get frozen looking too far back and too far forward, all at once. I often find myself at war with my memories, but somehow it all melds together into a messy compilation that is me. All of those moments in my rearview—the happy ones, the messy ones, the difficult-to-process ones—have made me who I am. Perhaps there isn't a perfect balance between living in the present and dwelling on what has already passed. Perhaps this is my lifelong compilation; lingering for a moment in those former years, then turning to focus on the blue sky up ahead, consciously taking in the moments happening right now before checking the rearview mirror again. Perhaps this is the long drive home.

My mixtapes have all been boxed up for many, many years now. Moments and memories tucked safely away, collecting dust in an old Birkenstock shoe box. But every now and then—twenty-eight years later—I hear a song and memories stir. They rise instantly to the surface, catching my breath. I know where I was, who I was with, how I felt in that moment…and suddenly I am right back in high school, driving along the empty dirt roads back home, my thoughts running wild as the tires roll fast and the wind whips through the open driver's window. I am lost here, in a kind of joyous melancholy, listening to the mixtape of my own life. And for a brief moment, I glance in the rearview mirror and find that the sky is a brilliant blue.

Demons – Imagine Dragons

Author: Valerie Rubin

Feeling chronically anxious, on edge, and trapped in a cycle of worst-case scenarios is an all-too-common experience. Many lie awake at night, tormented by memories, mistakes, and the relentless fear that something is fundamentally wrong with them. Despite doing all the "right things"— attending therapy, meditating, exercising, and even taking medication—long-term relief often feels out of reach. The weight of anxiety lingers, leaving a constant yearning for something that truly brings peace.

For those trapped in this cycle, it can feel like an inescapable reality. There is a mask worn in public—at work, with friends, even in moments of supposed relaxation. Beneath it, however, there is exhaustion, an invisible struggle that few acknowledge out loud. The world seems to move effortlessly around while internally, the weight of anxiety remains a crushing force.

That crushing force was once an all-consuming reality. The moment of realizing there was a way out did not come from a doctor's advice or a self-help book, but from a song— "Demons" by Imagine Dragons. Hearing it for the first time was like a jolt to the system. The lyrics, raw and haunting, spoke to something deeper.

The words resonated like nothing else had before. They exposed an unspoken truth: pain and struggle are not personal failings. Even those who seem to "have it all," like Dan Reynolds, the lead singer of Imagine Dragons, battle their own inner demons. The realization was profound—if someone like him, successful by all societal standards, could struggle, then perhaps the struggle wasn't a sign of brokenness after all.

For so long, emotions had been suppressed. Growing up in a household filled with chaos and emotional turmoil led to the belief that expressing needs or feelings was a burden. A father with multiple sclerosis and a brother with autism meant that survival required shrinking into the background, avoiding anything that might add to an already stressful environment. Suppressing emotions seemed like the only option.

But emotions, when ignored, have a way of resurfacing— often in the body. What began as headaches eventually spiraled into chronic pain, neck tension, and digestive issues. The stress never disappeared; instead, it manifested physically, much like a beach ball being held underwater. The longer it was suppressed, the stronger the force when it inevitably shot back up.

At its worst, the pain became debilitating. Walking up the stairs became impossible. A partner at the time would carry the weight of what had become an unrecognizable body. The experience was terrifying, not only for the physical toll but for the realization that it mirrored a painful family dynamic — a mother forced into the role of caretaker for a father. The fear of repeating that cycle felt inescapable.

For years, the belief persisted that the body had betrayed itself. But in reality, it had been holding on — doing its best to survive. A powerful quote from hypnotherapist Marisa Peer changed everything:

"The feeling that cannot find its expression in tears may cause other organs to weep."

The body had not been the enemy; it had been carrying unspoken pain, waiting to be heard.

Music had always been a source of comfort, but something about this particular song shifted everything. It wasn't just about the melody — it was about the permission it gave to feel, to acknowledge the struggle, and to recognize that healing was possible. Hearing *"I can't escape this now, unless you show me how"* became a turning point. It was a wake-up call that healing required something more.

Seeking therapy had been a long-standing habit, but something was missing. That's when a new path emerged — somatic therapy. Meeting Emily Colligan, a somatic coach, became the moment that changed everything. Up until that point, the mind had been the primary battleground, but the true root of anxiety had been in the body all along.

For those who have lived with chronic anxiety and trauma, the body often becomes an unsafe place. Disconnection becomes second nature. Thoughts race, overthinking intensifies, and the nervous system remains in a constant state of fight or flight. But through somatic therapy, things began to change. Slowly, the anxiety lessened. Within six months, the physical pain disappeared entirely. Life no longer felt like a constant battle. Presence, peace, and a genuine sense of self-worth replaced the endless cycle of fear.

It wasn't about simply "choosing positive thoughts," as so many self-help influencers suggest. Thoughts are not just a matter of willpower—they are deeply connected to the nervous system state. Healing required learning how to process emotions, regulate the nervous system, and, most importantly, reconnect with the body.

That realization led to a major shift. The plan to pursue a Ph.D. in clinical psychology no longer felt aligned. Traditional talk therapy had provided insights, but it hadn't provided true relief. Instead, the journey turned toward hypnotherapy and somatic therapy—methods that had brought actual transformation. A new understanding emerged:

When reactions feel overwhelming, they are often not coming from the rational, adult self. They are echoes of the inner child, perceiving old threats in new situations. Recognizing this changed everything.

That same year, something deeply personal came full circle—seeing Imagine Dragons perform live. Hearing "Demons" in person, the very song that had cracked open the door to healing, was surreal. When Dan Reynolds shared the personal struggles that inspired the song, it reinforced what had already been learned: no one is immune to pain, no matter how perfect life may look from the outside.

There is a tendency to believe that happiness will come after certain milestones—a degree, a successful career, a loving relationship. But the truth is, external achievements don't erase internal wounds. Trauma, anxiety, and depression don't magically disappear once success is reached. Healing is an internal process.

As Reynolds spoke about his own struggles and the impact of therapy, it was a reminder that healing is universal. The struggles that once felt isolating were, in reality, shared by so many. The old belief that success equals happiness shattered. True happiness isn't found in external accomplishments—it comes from within.

Music has a way of opening doors that logic alone cannot. It can validate emotions, create connection, and spark transformation. "Demons" was more than just a song—it was a lifeline, a catalyst for healing, and a reminder that no one is ever truly alone in their pain.

Healing isn't about erasing struggle; it's about learning to navigate it. When trauma is released, when emotions are allowed to be felt, and when the nervous system finds regulation, life becomes something different—something lighter, freer. The external world may still be chaotic, but inner peace becomes unshakable.

The ego insists that happiness will come after something is achieved. The soul, however, knows the truth: once peace is found within, everything else will fall into place.

Anyway – Martina McBride

Author: Lana Ryder

""I Sing, I Dream, I Love... Anyway."

The song "Anyway" by Martina McBride continues to be a source of hope and encouragement for me. It speaks to anyone walking through deep heartache, loss, or rejection. More than anything, it reminds us that no matter what we face—or how broken we feel—we can keep going. We can choose to go on, *anyway*.

The first time I heard it, the proverbial rug was pulled out from under me, and I began sobbing. I broke.

Luckily, I had just gotten into my car and was parked. As I often do when music hits me deep, I stopped everything and listened. This—this was not just a song. It felt like a message from Spirit, from Love, from Healing itself. I hadn't even realized how much I needed it until that moment.

The protective wall I had built around my heart—the one that kept me from fully grieving all that had been lost—collapsed with the power of the opening lines.

I bought the CD and listened to it again. I heard more than just a melody. I felt the hope and intention embedded in the lyrics. I heard the soul of the creators in the progressions, the chords, the phrasing. And I felt it all come alive through Martina McBride's extraordinary voice, rich with both compassion and conviction.

She sings about how you can spend your whole life building something from nothing, and how one storm can take it all away. And yet, you *build it anyway*.

That line didn't speak to career or external achievements for me—it spoke to the home and the family my husband and I had built over thirty-five years. Two young kids who got married before they were ready, trying to raise a family the best way they knew how. It wasn't always easy. There were painful challenges and regrets—but there was also goodness. Joy. Sweet, beautiful memories. There was Love. And then, there was divorce.

I didn't see it coming. I believed things were finally heading in a bright new direction. That's why Martina's next verse hit so hard. She sings about how you can love someone with all your heart, for all the right reasons, and in a moment, they can walk away. But still—you *love them anyway*.

This song reached into my deepest grief and offered it back to me as a kind of blessing.

I think about this a lot when I look at the world around us. The anger, the division, the need to be right at the expense of connection. So many seem to forget what matters: that we belong to each other, that healing starts by listening. By caring. By showing up.

And yet, even amid that division, I still believe.

When I get discouraged by what I see in the world, I speak it aloud: I still believe in a better world. It may not arrive in my lifetime, but I will keep holding that vision. I will keep using music, voice, and love to teach, to heal, to connect. I've seen people of every background come together through music. I've seen it bridge divides.

And so, I will continue. For my children. My grandchildren. For your children. For all of us. Anyway.

Crawling – Linkin Park

Author: Michelle Wolfe

I was so angry.

I had so much rage.

There I was, in the throes of PTSD symptoms—flashbacks, intrusive thoughts, emotional turbulence, panic attacks. *Crawling in my skin.* It was all-consuming, an endless loop of pain I couldn't escape.

At the edge of 21, I was utterly lost, my mental health deteriorating. In college, and for most of my adolescent life, I lived unconsciously, numbing myself with self-abuse and self-abandonment. Low self-esteem and traumatic experiences fueled my choices, and I burned through them recklessly. Society expects you to step seamlessly into adulthood—to find a job, a partner, maybe start a family— but I felt like I didn't have a clue.

"Crawling in my skin, these wounds, they will not heal." I was still carrying the weight of trauma, and I wasn't ready to confront it. Not until I had my first child at 29 did I begin to wake up to who I was meant to be. That was when I started to gain the self-awareness I had been missing so I could see my patterns with greater clarity.

I vividly remember a conversation with a therapist friend about triggers. She explained what they are and how to identify them. At the time, I didn't realize how disconnected I was from my body, how numb I had become. Back then, the sensation of *crawling in my skin* wasn't just a lyric—it was my reality. That phrase so perfectly described the visceral discomfort, the relentless unease of living with unresolved trauma.

I know what it's like to sit in the dark, trapped in your thoughts. To feel as though no one can really help you. To want to disappear. To feel like you shouldn't even exist.

I know what it's like to have a mind that feeds you lies. Lies that tell you you're unworthy, undeserving, that you've done too much wrong to ever find redemption. Lies that tell you you're a burden.

For years, I carried guilt and shame like a second skin. It began in early childhood, rooted in sexual trauma, and grew heavier with time. I perpetuated my own shame through choices I knew were wrong—giving myself away to people who hadn't earned it, didn't deserve it. I made decisions I regretted, knowing they weren't in alignment with who I wanted to be. Shame is isolating; it traps you in cycles of escapism, bad behaviors, and reactivity.

Healing shame is hard. It requires vulnerability—sharing your darkest moments with safe people in safe spaces.

For me, shame often manifested as anger. I couldn't ignore it anymore. My son was four, and I was struggling to manage my emotions. Too often, I lost my temper with him, snapping or yelling in ways that broke my heart. He didn't deserve that, and I hated myself for it. One day, I walked into a therapist's office and said, *"I need help with my anger."*

One of the most valuable lessons I learned in therapy was that anger is an umbrella emotion. Beneath it lies something deeper. My therapist encouraged me to pause when I felt the anger rise and ask myself, *"What's underneath this?"*

The first time I did, the answer was clear: helplessness. I felt helpless as a parent, overwhelmed by the weight of responsibility. I didn't know what I was doing and had no healthy examples to draw from. Instead, I had a map of what not to do. That helplessness fueled my frustration and disconnected me from my son's experience of me. It reinforced fear, which only added to my guilt and shame.

But recognizing this was the turning point. I realized I didn't want to perpetuate the cycles of my past. I sought help to better manage my anger and repair my relationship with my son.

That little boy who was four when I first sought help is now about to turn fourteen. He's taller than me, proud to call me "shorty," and loves to flex his height advantage. But I'll always see the boy who saved me. He woke me up. His presence forced me to confront my trauma, my patterns, and the pain I hadn't addressed. It was because of him that I started to become really conscious of who I am, what I had been through, and how I was showing up in the world.

Music became a lifeline during those dark years. When the emotions I carried were too big to contain, I turned to "Crawling" and other songs by Linkin Park. I'd blast them in my car, Chester Bennington's voice pouring through the speakers, and scream along until the weight in my chest felt lighter. His haunting delivery mirrored the chaos I felt inside, giving me permission to let it out. Depression, anger, seething beneath the surface.

The lyrics were a lifeline: *"Crawling in my skin, these wounds, they will not heal."* They captured the relentless pain, the shame, the need for release. Singing along with the music gave me a way to process emotions I couldn't otherwise express. Chester's hauntingly beautiful and emotionally evocative voice felt like he was screaming for me, saying the words I couldn't find. He spent his career pouring his pain into his music, giving voice to the struggles so many of us face. His loss is heartbreaking, a stark reminder of how deep that pain can run. And yet, in that awareness, I find my own reason to stay. His music carried me through the darkness, and even now, his absence reminds me of the preciousness of life—the very thing he fought so hard to hold onto.

For years, the entire *Hybrid Theory* album was my cathartic outlet. It allowed me to pour out my rage and sadness, to feel the things I had numbed for so long. But recently, something shifted, and I noticed when the song "Crawling" came on, and it didn't hit the same. The familiar wave of emotions didn't rise. I wasn't numb—I was healed. The heaviness that had once consumed me was gone.

That realization was profound. It reminded me that music evolves with us. A song that once felt like a lifeline can become a marker of growth. It reflects the person you were when you first heard it and the person you've become since. "Crawling" will always hold a sacred place in my heart, but today, it reminds me of how far I've come.

Music has that power. It connects us to emotions we can't always name, inviting us to dive deeper into our pain and then offering a way out.

I'm grateful this song no longer carries the emotional weight it once did. But I'll never forget how it carried me when I needed it most.

Hold Back the River - James Bay

Author: Jennifer Eggerts

This song has become a spell for me. It contains years of hopes, dreams and anticipatory energy. It is on no less than half a dozen playlists and it has both haunted and animated me in countless ways over the years.

Why?

I have always been the river.

A force of nature; uncontrollable, wild and unyielding. I was the child who ran with fairies, spoke with God(dess) and talked to animals. It wasn't until I entered Kindergarten that I have any memory of these being negative attributes. I knew that there was a difference between those of us who were "alive" and those of us who were not. Though I may never be completely sure, I am relatively confident that I was a pretty skilled medium at age two. The first time this realization hit my consciousness, I was in my late thirties and I about fell out of my chair. I was at work at the time and had a client come in who also happened to be psychic. What makes this story even funnier is that we both worked for a Glass Franchising company and it was an extremely zipped up professional environment.

It's not just the life that flourishes around me. It is also the torrent of life and power running through me that has been enough to drive me within an inch of complete insanity. I have never lacked for ebullience, eloquence or excellence in my natural balanced state. To say that I have often pictured myself as too much would be an understatement. My "river" has rarely been well received in structured, rule driven society. I stick out like a sore thumb and have often found myself the target of hate, shame and ridicule. Something about me also provides a clear mirror to people and they see the parts that they MOST need to see and those parts are not always pretty.

The first time I heard the song, I was driving in my car in Southern California. I was running a sober living facility, barely a year and a half sober myself. I had finally learned to 'button up' the parts of me that did not fit in "recovery" or in real life. Being a torrent of raw power and joy has had its drawbacks and they are considerable.

At that point I was just beginning to come to terms with the fact that I, Jen Eggerts, did more damage to myself than any other perpetrator. I was starting to really lean into the fact that, while necessary for survival, I had still abandoned parts of myself on the side of the road like trash. The opening stanza of the song just about took the air completely from my lungs. I tried SO DESPERATELY to get better, to save myself from my demons, to play nice with capitalism, to love a man who couldn't love me back. I tried to keep all of it close to me, but life did get in the way and I became the casualty of the war. Over and over again.

It took 33 years of "life" to dam me up to the point of complete shutdown. That feeling, of being completely blocked off from myself, with my life in complete shambles, is one I never want to feel again. The cost of actually holding back the river is too high and this song has also become a symbol of actually letting the river flow return to me. I have wanted to just let the river rush through me for years. I regularly ask myself just where I am still holding back the river. So often I can feel the places that are still dammed (and damned). As the beat of the song drums, it lights my body up enough to generate a hum in the places where life has ceased.

It has been a simple recitation that I sing to myself:

"*Hold back the river,*" I whisper, just for a moment—so I can stop, see myself clearly, and offer what was once missing.

In those lines, I feel myself calling to every age I've ever been, to the Jen that hid when it didn't feel safe to shine. These words are my invitation to all the hurt, silenced parts of me: Come into the light. You belong.

When I first began listening to the song, the idea of looking into my own eyes—or holding myself with compassion—felt impossible. But I could sense it. I could see the future version of me who could. Even at my lowest, something in me knew:

I wasn't going through all of this for nothing. There had to be a homecoming waiting for me on the other side.

The song became more than music—it became a symbol of reunion. A reminder that I didn't come here to live a small life. I came to feel—to let the river flow freely, with all its force and beauty.

In these words, I whisper to all of the hidden parts of me that are still in pain and invite them into the light and into my life. I no longer seek to fight against the tide or hold myself at bay. This has been a slow process as well.

When I first started listening to the song, I hated myself. The thought of being able to look in my own eyes, let alone hold myself seemed like an impossibility. I could see it, though. I could feel it. I knew it was coming. There was no way in hell that I was going to go through what I had been through (what I continue to go through) without there being some powerful and rich homecoming. I decided a long time ago that I wasn't particularly inclined to settle for a small life.

I want joy. I want deep, loving connections. I want to feel the water washing through me with wild abandon. I am currently 44 years old and coming off a period of intense pain, reckoning, growth, and healing. It has been a tremendously difficult four years that have often felt insurmountable. At times, I have been unsure of whether or not I was going to make it.

Here's the thing though – I am not a quitter and I have worked my ass off to get this far. Sometimes I am the river, sometimes the river is coming at me and sometimes the river flows through me. I have already lived several different lives and traversed parts of the human condition many don't come back from. I am genuinely hoping that the next couple of decades are far less painful than the last few. Regardless, I am here to bear witness, to evolve in and with compassion, to teach and to love harder.

Something I have learned over the years is just how much of the human journey is held inside our subconscious. For whatever reason, I have never been particularly skilled at keeping my subconscious from bubbling over into reality. Maybe it is because of my neurodivergent sensitivity. Maybe it is because of the wicked psychic abilities. Maybe it's all the trauma. Maybe it is all of it, Maybe it is none of it.

Regardless, we are not meant to toil in such painful lives. The human condition, at least in my opinion, is something to be celebrated for its diversity. We are meant to relish in our differences and to play inside the many varieties of creativity. I also know that the world that we live in is not at all appreciative or accommodating of those of us that have the courage and audacity to dream; especially those of us who are incapable of conforming to situations and structures that cause us harm. Our climate and ways of life are changing whether we acknowledge it or not. Either we find more sustainable ways of living or Gaia may boot us straight off the planet.

I am so incredibly tired of holding back the river; personally, relationally, professionally and collectively. When I started to write this entry, this was not at all the prose I expected to find on the page. Alas, sometimes writing has a tendency to take on a life of its own. I am so incredibly fortunate to be one of those individuals who can take life in fully. The reverse is also true in the fact that I often take in the most unfortunate parts of the human condition. In the last few years, it has become incredibly evident to me that we are on the edge of major collective change. In the ways that I no longer want to hold back the river, I am finding that so many others share the same desire to embrace more life with far less conditionality placed upon us. We are ready for something more because we are something more.

I often also picture my nieces and nephews as I listen to this song. I hope and pray that they do not have to hold back the river in the ways that I have. I hope and pray that the wisdom from my troubles can be imparted to them in a way that they never have to experience the same. I hope that my generation and the generations that are coming behind can help unravel and solve the great issues of our time. I want the children of tomorrow to have a healthy planet, with healthy systems and governments that can support them.

I want them to lean into their rivers. I want them to bring into the power that runs through their veins and celebrate their inner voices.

May we also learn to slow down the river long enough to appreciate each other. May we fill the lonely water with our laughter and tears as we share in the beautiful mess that is the human condition. We are not without hope.

Vica Versa – Pastor Troy

Author: Kimberly Belk

Throughout our lives, we often find ourselves grappling with the complexities of human relationships and self-discovery. Like a ship navigating stormy waters; we seek solace and understanding amidst the chaos that surrounds us. In the song "Vica Versa" by Pastor Troy, the lyrics resonate deeply with my own journey of introspection and spiritual awakening.

Growing up in a Catholic household, I was taught that God was all-powerful, all-seeing, and, above all, to be feared. From a young age, I internalized the belief that every mistake and every moral misstep could have eternal consequences. This fear was not just theoretical; it was visceral. I remember the paralyzing anxiety I felt whenever I contemplated sinning or falling short of the moral expectations laid out for me. The idea of an all-loving God seemed contradictory to the constant fear of punishment that loomed over my every action.

This fear was particularly poignant when it came to my older sister, who is a lesbian. According to the teachings I grew up with, her very identity was seen as a grave sin, and one that could potentially condemn her to hell. The thought of my sister, someone I loved deeply, burning in hell for simply being who she was, filled me with terror. Yet, as I grew older, I began to question the narrative I had been taught. The God I was beginning to know and understand felt different from the punitive figure I had been raised to fear. This God was all-loving, compassionate, and accepting—a far cry from the wrathful deity I had been taught to worship. This growing awareness sparked an internal conflict: Who taught us to fear God, and why?

As my twin sister and I navigated our lives, we found ourselves increasingly at odds with the Catholic ideals we were raised with. Between us, we had five children, each with a different father. In the eyes of the church, and many within our religious community, this was a mark of shame – a failure to live up to the expectations of what a "good" Catholic woman should be. The judgment we faced was harsh, and the sense of not fitting in grew stronger with each passing year.

The Catholic household we grew up in was steeped in tradition and strict moral codes, leaving little room for deviation from the norm. As young mothers, our lives did not fit the mold. The expectation was clear: to be a "good" Catholic, one must adhere to certain standards, including chastity before marriage and a stable, nuclear family. Our lives, with their complexities and challenges, simply did not align with these ideals.

The judgment and alienation we experienced from our religious community was painful. We were looked down upon, whispered about, and made to feel as though we were less than others. This judgment extended beyond us to our children, who, through no fault of their own, were also seen as products of our supposed moral failings. The shame and guilt were overwhelming at times, leading to a profound sense of isolation. It was during this time that I began to see the cracks in the façade of religious righteousness. The very people who were supposed to embody love, compassion, and forgiveness were often the first to cast stones.

My twin sister's journey was particularly difficult. To support her family, she made the decision to work as a stripper. In the eyes of many, this was a morally reprehensible choice, one that brought further shame upon our family. The societal norms we grew up with dictated that a "good" woman did not engage in such work, and the religious community was quick to judge. The shame associated with her decision was immense, and the weight of societal expectations bore down heavily on her.

Yet, it was within this very environment, so often condemned by society, that my sister found some of the most amazing and kind-hearted people she had ever known. The individuals she worked with at the club were supportive, compassionate, and non-judgmental. They understood her situation, respected her choices, and offered her the kind of camaraderie and kindness that was sorely lacking from those who judged her at church. This stark contrast between the judgmental attitudes of the so-called "righteous" and the genuine kindness of those who worked in an environment deemed "immoral" opened my eyes to the complexities of human morality.

It became clear to me that the binary notions of good and evil, right and wrong, were far more nuanced than I had been led to believe. The people at the club, who were often dismissed as sinners by society, exhibited the very qualities of compassion, empathy, and generosity that I had been taught to associate with holiness. This realization was both liberating and troubling, as it forced me to confront the contradictions in my beliefs and the way I perceived the world.

My marriage in 2008 to a man struggling with drug addiction further challenged my understanding of morality and goodness. Addiction is a brutal, relentless force, one that consumes not only the individual struggling with it but also those who love and care for them. My husband, despite his flaws and the destructive nature of his addiction, was still someone I loved deeply. His addiction brought immense pain into our lives, yet I could not bring myself to abandon him, even as his choices hurt both him and those around him.

As I witnessed the devastation that addiction wreaked on my husband and those around him, I also saw the compassion and generosity of the people who struggled with it. Many of my friends, who also battled addiction, were some of the most giving and kind-hearted individuals I had ever known.

They would give you the shirt off their back if you needed it, even if they had nothing to spare. Their struggles with addiction did not diminish their humanity; if anything, it seemed to amplify their empathy for others in pain.

In contrast, I saw how so-called "good" people, those who adhered to societal norms and religious expectations, often turned a blind eye to the suffering of those battling addiction. These "good" people, who attended church regularly and upheld the values of the community, were often quick to judge and slow to help. This paradox was deeply unsettling. How could those who were supposed to embody the values of compassion and love be so indifferent to the suffering of others? And how could those who were condemned as sinners exhibit such profound generosity and kindness?

These experiences led me to question everything I had been taught about morality, good, and evil. The lines between these concepts became increasingly blurred, and I found myself in a place of deep introspection. The idea that goodness could be found in places and people that society condemned, and that evil could lurk within the hearts of those deemed righteous, was a profound revelation.

As I delved deeper into the lyrics of "Vica Versa," I realized that Pastor Troy was grappling with the same questions that had been plaguing me. The song challenges the listener to reconsider their preconceived notions of good and evil, right and wrong. What if everything we deemed virtuous was, in reality, tainted with malevolence? What if heaven resided not in the skies above, but within the very fabric of our earthly existence? These questions resonated deeply with me as I reflected on my own experiences.

The song's exploration of duality and balance echoed the ancient philosophies and scriptures that speak of the necessity of equilibrium in all things. Just as light cannot exist without darkness, good cannot exist without evil. This concept of yin and yang, of the interconnectedness of opposites, began to make sense to me in a way it never had before. The angels depicted in the Bible, beings of divine purity, were often described as both awe-inspiring and fearsome. It is our human perception that imbues them with angelic qualities, blurring the lines between good and evil.

As I reflected on the profound message of "Vica Versa," I realized that my understanding of morality, good, and evil had evolved. I was moving away from the black-and-white morality of my upbringing towards a more nuanced view. I began to see that true beauty lies not in the absence of flaws, but in the harmonious interplay of light and shadow. Through embracing our contradictions and shedding the shackles of societal norms, we can unearth a paradise within our own hearts and minds. By transcending the limitations of duality, we pave the way for a world where heaven and earth intertwine, creating a tapestry of existence that is both flawed and sublime.

Pastor Troy's "Vica Versa" serves as a poignant reminder of the intricate dance of good and evil within us all. It challenges us to look beyond surface judgments and embrace the inherent contradictions that define our humanity. Just as God encompasses both light and darkness, so too can we find beauty in the most unexpected places. By embracing the paradoxes of our existence, we can cultivate a heaven on earth that transcends the confines of conventional morality.

In my own life, I have found that the path to true spiritual awakening lies in the acceptance of these contradictions. By moving beyond the rigid moral codes of my upbringing, I have discovered a deeper, more authentic connection to the divine. I have come to understand that heaven and hell are not distant, otherworldly realms, but states of being that we create through our thoughts, actions, and perceptions.

In the end, it is not about fitting into the mold that society or religion has created for us. It is about finding balance within ourselves, embracing our flaws, and recognizing the beauty in our imperfections. By doing so, we can create a personal heaven on earth, a place of peace, love, and understanding that transcends the dualities of good and evil. This, I believe, is the true message of "Vica Versa."

Would? – Alice in Chains

Author: Matthew Solomon

It was early Summer of 1992. I had just finished my first year of college at the University of Southern California School of Music. I had long hair, played guitar, and was incredibly shy—especially around women. And, I had just experienced my first real heartbreak.

She was a little older than me, we knew each other through mutual friends, I really liked her, and we romantically connected two weeks before she moved to Hawaii for good. I went from the happiest I had ever remembered being, to feeling like my guts had been ripped out the day she left. I had fantasies about making my way to Hawaii to be together, until I heard she got engaged to someone on the Island two months later. I was incredibly depressed, felt completely rejected, and hated myself.

The Dirt album by Alice in Chains came out that summer, and I listened to it on repeat for probably 3-4 months straight. It was the perfect soundtrack for what I was going through—from the opening song, "Them Bones" through to the closing song "Would?," I took that sonic journey over and over again, trying to process and redirect all of my grief. I wrote songs and lyrics inspired by this album and was doing all I could to direct my angst into my music. I knew the songs were about drugs – I mean "Junkhead?" And while I did not do drugs, I don't even think I had smoked weed yet, I could relate to the excruciating emotional pain that permeated the album.

I loved all of Dirt, but "Would?" was the one song that, when asked about my desert island playlist, would be at the top. I still listen to it on repeat and recite the lyrics whenever I am getting physically, mentally, or emotionally thrashed.

I started surfing in 2004. My friend and I would go to the beach, paddle out, get tossed around, and make our way back out until we had no fight left. Paddling back out into the daunting waves, one of us would usually start singing, *"Into the flood again..."*

Going through my divorce in 2012, having to deal with child custody mediation, legal processes, and trying to keep my head up, I would often sing to myself, *"Into the flood again...try to see it once my way"* Indeed, being understood is one of those things that are so important to me. In fact, one of my closest friends told me that's my weakness. So, of course, "try to see it once my way," would be a constant in my life.

Traversing dating post-divorce, and trying to stay positive and move on, with hope, those same lyrics were always playing in my head.

They also applied to my work, going from job to job, project to project, and rejection to possibility. Over and over again, I went "into the flood again." When something seemed really promising, and like I was getting close to a big breakthrough, I'd ask myself, *"If I would, could you?"*

Musically, I also geek out on how there is so much happening in this song. Ever present are the growling bass intro, the deliberate and powerful rolling thunder of the drums, the sparse and dissonant guitars, and those haunting vocal harmonies that are so very Alice in Chains. I read somewhere that Alice in Chains were referred to as "the Satanic Everly Brothers" because of how their voices worked and sounded together, and I have not been able to unhear that. Alice in Chains had a whole vibe, and "Would?" is that perfect song of theirs.

The reality is, 90s grunge and Hip Hop have been the soundtrack for my life since the actual 90s. There are so many songs that have kept me going and given me inspiration during my time as a filmmaker and in my work facilitating conflict resolution. As Kurt Cobain declared in "Serve the Servants." "Teenage angst has [really] paid off well." I don't mean "paid off well" for me monetarily, but in terms of feeding and nourishing me while providing that much needed outlet to rage when I needed to and to release my anger, anxiety, and depression in the moments I have experienced them. But even with that long list of songs on my angsty playlist, when I hear the growling bass intro of "Would?" – I still feel exhilarated…and understood.

Help Me to Feel Again – Judah and the Lion

Author: Becca Zelner

*To my sweet Meghan. I will always cherish you.

Ah, this one hits me in the feels right away. This song is one of those that will always bring me to tears when I'm having a bad day (or sometimes a good day).

I lost my very best friend last year. She got kind of sick and eventually it progressed so much that her organs shut down. She was in the hospital for about a week before she eventually passed away. Devastated isn't even the right word. I felt like I lost an entire part of myself.

We met when we were just young adults working at a local restaurant. I had already been there for a few months when she walked through the door. I instantly knew that we were meant to be friends. It was like we clicked automatically. That first night we went to the bar, had a few drinks, and a forever friendship was born. And my goodness were we the real genuine type of friends too…the laughs, the heartache, the successes, and even the sorrows.

Meghan was always there.

When she first moved to the area, she lived in this little house in town with a crazy roommate and her dog, Spike – the cutest rescue pit bull in the world. She hosted all kinds of firepit nights and day parties at her place. It made us grow so close, so fast. It became a very regular routine for the two of us – go to work, go to her house, have a drink or two, and go out at night. However, the both of us both lived "other lives," working and going to school, but we always had time for each other. I have an entire lifetime of memories with her and boy, were those some serious stories.

Meghan went to buy a house because she was unhappy with her living situation. What's more, when she finally bought her house, I was the first person she called. She was so excited that she was adulting and doing grown-up things. I went to her new house (which was empty, except for a lawn chair in her living room) and told her she at least needed a hand towel. We laughed and carried on about how excited we were for this next phase of her life. And we ran to the store and got her a hand towel. Simple pleasures.

Not that we were not close before, but after she bought the house, our friendship really bloomed. She was always my go-to gal for what I needed, and I was that for her, too. Her house had a pool and it was in bad shape when she bought it. The water was green, it was dirty, and it needed a lot of work. Well, don't you know that spring, we put in the work, and every year after that, it was our spring ritual to get the pool ready for summer.

Her family was always at her house, which made me close with them, too. When my nephew was born, he had a birthing injury. It was a horrible few weeks. He's healthy and thriving now, thank goodness. Anyway, after being so worried about him, her family always knew how to comfort me. They'd pray for me (not my thing) but it felt good anyway. That's the type of people that they are. That's the type of woman that they raised. That was Meghan.

When the pandemic hit, we spent nearly that entire summer together, and then all the summers after that. We hung out besides the summertime, but it was so easy with Meghan. We could show up if we wanted to. We could swim whenever we wanted. She would go to football games with us and we would go to her house to watch. It was a great give and take, reciprocal relationship.

I'll always remember the regular phone calls from her to tell me about a creepy man she saw driving or how the girl at the coffee shop spelled her name wrong.

In 2022, Meghan sold her house. She moved back in with her parents. She never told me why she felt like she needed to move back, but it didn't matter. I still loved and supported her. The first summer without her was weird, but I always knew that I could count on her.

Our friendship had lasted through so much heartbreak and hardship that it didn't matter where she was. I think that's why this will always hurt so much.

I got a notice that she was in the hospital in January 2023. I asked her mom how she was doing. At the time, it wasn't horrible. But that quickly changed....VERY quickly. Meghan was sick, really *really* sick. Before they knew it, Meghan was in a coma and before long, she was gone. Meghan went into multiple organ failure and she couldn't get better.

To say I was devastated is an understatement. I cannot tell you the last time it felt like my soul was actually taken out of my body for a second. It was the absolute worst feeling in the world. My best friend in the entire world was gone. My one constant in my life since I was 19. Ten years of friendship....

I had to somehow stomach going to Meghan's funeral, which was arguably the second worst day since she had passed. It was absolutely gut wrenching to watch all of her closest loved ones gathered together and mourning. This wasn't Meg. She was always the happiest person I knew – the one I could call for a smile or a laugh. And there we were, crying and sad. There is nothing to prepare you for watching your best friend get buried.

For weeks, nothing helped. I tried to do all of the things that we did together to keep her memory alive, as if it never happened. We ate mango habañero wings from her favorite place, had drinks that reminded us of her, and looked at pictures... memories of our time together. Still, nothing helped. I still really missed her.

I turned to the one thing that I thought could help – music. It did at first, sometimes. This song – "Help Me to Feel Again" – helped the most. I needed the words. I needed something to finally break through. I needed something to help me feel again. The band claims that the song was written following the pandemic after some therapy sessions that they had. The advice during therapy was to allow you to express your feelings and not bottle things up because it comes back to bite you later. This is the purpose of the song.

Music, but particularly this song, helped me heal. It helped me realize the feelings that I was feeling were real and that it was okay to feel them. It also helped me recognize that I needed to talk about her and her legacy. Once I realized how important it was to begin to let go, it got better. Letting go doesn't mean forgetting, letting go means beginning to heal and beginning to feel. I listened to this song a lot trying to realize the importance of feeling again and beginning to let myself heal from heartbreak. The craziest thing about heartbreak is that it doesn't always come from romantic love. Heartbreak can come from love that is from a friend, love that feels real and normal and warming.

I miss Meghan every single day. There isn't a single day that goes by that I don't think about her and our friendship. I miss her hugs and her voice and her laugh. I miss the crazy phone calls and humorous text messages. None of that will ever come back. But the memories will always help me to remember her.

Part 2: Growth, Resilience, & The Bonds That Shape Us

Relationships, connection, love, and longing

"Music expresses that which cannot be put into words and that which cannot remain silent." – Victor Hugo

Wish You Were Here - Incubus

Author: Becca Zelner

Life is full of unexpected adventures. It can be big successes or devastating losses. It is all about how you handle those wins and losses and what you decide to do with them to make your life more fulfilling. I can remember times when I wished there were people there to celebrate with me. And it's weird how your successes come in different waves. Think about your last "success" and if it was at work, at home, with your partner, with your child. Was it so great that you wanted to share it with others? Who was there with you? Do you wish that there was someone else there instead? Who do you call when you need to share?

I am the happiest when I am relaxing at the beach, but who isn't? Toes in the sand, the mind is able to just relax and wander. But wandering can be dangerous. Wandering can lead to hours of sadness and confusion. We don't talk enough about difficult life events, especially when they happen before your brain is fully formed to make a decision about it; as if the case with childhood trauma.

My parents divorced when I was seven, though it felt like they were divorced long before that time. My memories of them being together are mostly gone, with the exception of some silly moments which still remain. The divorce was rough for all of us except for my dad. His issues were deep rooted, and he may not have realized the harm his behaviors caused. I needed verbal affirmation from him – I always have.

I have always wished that I could get that validation from him. Just one time.

The song "Wish You Were Here" by Incubus means more to me that can be expressed. I wish he had been there for so many of my moments. I wish that our relationship was simpler, and his presence was felt. I never realized that I would be wishing for someone to be here when they are, well, still here. It feels impossible that I am wishing for someone who is here to be... here. And maybe that's selfish. There are people who miss their loved ones every single day because they aren't here physically. Yet, here I am, wishing for someone to be present with me who is still alive.

I tried so many times to replace the love that was missing in my life. I was so lucky that I had a step-parent who loved me like his own. It was the first time that I felt that sense of father figure in my life. But, no matter what, I always wanted a dad. Not just any dad. The dads you see on TV. The father/daughter relationships that make you jealous. The dad who walks his daughter down the aisle and cries. The dad who shows up to catch a mouse. The dad who comes and fixes things in your house. And I missed all of that. I missed the dependable dad. I missed the comparison photos of us as adults and us as younger versions of ourselves.

I guess I never understood why I couldn't have all those things with my dad. For a large part of my teenage/early adult life I thought it was my fault. As if I was the one that wasn't good enough to deserve this type of love or maybe that type of love didn't really exist. As if all of the father/daughter relationships you saw on TV were fake.

I think that the purpose of this song is to imagine that those who you love (or long for) the most are there in your greatest achievements and your greatest failures. But maybe it's also focusing on those who literally are not here. Isn't that the beauty of music? Our own interpretation?

Maybe it is those who are not here with us anymore. Maybe it is about wishing that those who are in another world are here with us every single day.

If that's the case, I would wish for my grandmother. Quite honestly, my grandmother was the most selfless and beautiful person that I knew. WOW, would she be so proud of us kids and of being a great-grandmother. I think about all of the things that she missed and realize how lucky I am that I got her for such important parts of my life. She missed so many big things though, too. My high school and college graduations, my wedding, my career, my education, and my current life. And you know, my grandfather is still here, and I completely recognize how lucky I am to have him (still!).

Losing my grandmother was so weird because I felt like I lost a part of myself, too. I swear she is the reason why I love to read. And why I dedicated myself and my life to my education and my career. Not to mention, losing someone of such significance this early in your life impacts you forever.

This band is one of those bands that writes music that feels like it sits with you for an eternity. It's one of those songs that once you hear it, you know it's going to come back again and again. I feel like it's important to tell you about one of the first times I heard this in concert because it was one of those life-changing moments that I will never forget.

The year was 2017. We were getting ready to see Incubus in Camden, NJ at the Pavilion. It was July and we knew that it was going to be hot – and it was! We tailgated in the parking lot for a couple of hours and headed to the lawn to get ready to rock out. Incubus played and they were just as incredible as I could have ever imagined.

As fate would have it, this concert happened on the same day that Chester Bennington (of Linkin' Park) had died. It was a true shock to the punk world. Anyone who grew up listening to the likes of Incubus, etc. also listened to Linkin' Park. When Brandon Boyd grabbed the microphone to sing this song, he dedicated it to Chester. And when I tell you there wasn't a dry eye in the house, I mean it. We all felt it in our own way. Whether or not that was longing for someone we love, or sad about Chester, or truly wishing that someone was there with us in that moment; we all felt the pain of loss.

It took me the longest amount of time to realize that I was allowed to be happy and sad at the same time. I got the word *"saudade"* tattooed on my inner arm. It means "longing" in Portuguese. Although there is no direct translation, it's melancholic longing, yearning – desiderium.

There is no "cure" to this feeling. The feeling is permanent missing, longing, yearning. Does it get easier? Sometimes. That's what we hope for.

Grief will hurt us in all sorts of ways, and some of us are better at dealing with it than others. Wishing someone was still here, that they would come back or wishing to have more time with them are desires even long after someone has passed.

Music has a funny way of doing that. It can evoke many different feelings even within the same song. That's why it's the greatest form of art. It's a reminder that words and thoughts are put to paper, just like this, but formed into a tune that you hum in your shower or jam to in your car. It's a testament that a song can save your life or wish you had another chance to tell someone how you feel. That's what music does to you. That's what this song did to me.

I'll Stand By You – The Pretenders

Author: Joie Costa

I was raised on the promise of loyalty, the kind of loyalty that "I'll Stand By You" by The Pretenders captures so vividly. "When you don't know what to do... I'll stand by you" and I "won't let nobody hurt you." These words became the anthem of my heart, and a blueprint for the kind of love I both desired and attempted to give.

From a young age, I was taught that love meant having someone's back, no matter what. I grew up in the Bronx, NY during the mid-70s to the midmid-90s. The ride-or-die narrative was ingrained in me from a cultural Italian and Irish New York standpoint, and these were the street smart narratives I adopted. Not coincidentally, it was the quite random outlaw country musical taste my city-raised mother played at home. If love was hard, painful, enduring, and had to do with life and death, it made sense to me. To love someone was to be their unwavering support, their sanctuary in the storm.

The idea was intoxicating, a romanticized vision of love that felt like a calling. A sacred pact. A blood oath. Secure. *"Nothing you confess could make me love you less,"* the song promised, and I desperately wanted to be loved like that. I received this type of loyalty and commitment from my single mom as well and was often a bystander or witness of the loyalty above all mentality of street gangs and dysfunctional families. But in my quest to embody this ideal, I overlooked a crucial aspect of love: reciprocity. My fascination with this type of unwavering loyalty led me to offer it unconditionally, often to those who couldn't or wouldn't return it. I became a beacon for the unlovable, the dark, the misunderstood. My heart opened wide, ready to absorb their pain and offer solace.

Unconditional loyalty is not actually unconditional love.

In hindsight, unconditional love has never hurt me. Unconditional loyalty, however, has wounded me to the core because I was ungrounded and looking for someone to love me. The people who I thought were most loyal were actually just terrified of never having anyone else look at them the way I did. I saw their beauty, their potential, and validated their worth. And that is what I wanted. To be validated. To be seen as valuable and for someone to promise to love me no matter what.

I'd always felt like an alien of sorts and I believed, as I write this now in hindsight, that if I could find someone to stand by me it would prove I was not only human, but a human worth going into the dark for.

I found myself drawn to emotionally unavailable people, those who were not in other relationships for good reason.

Openly wounded people carrying shadows they couldn't face alone. My loyalty became an addiction for them, a space where they could unload their darkest, unshared parts. *"I'll stand by you, even your darkest hour,"* the song echoed in my mind, and I stood firm, even as their darkness seeped into me.

Love songs like "I'll Stand By You" romanticize this unwavering support, but they don't tell the whole story. They don't warn you about the toll it can take on your heart, the way it can erode your sense of self if you're not careful.

In seeking to be everything for someone else, I lost sight of the importance of being something for myself. I didn't know how to show myself the same sacred, forgiving compassion I offered to others. There is no way to create a shared experience alone, and yet I tried, over and over, until I was drained.

Then one day, I was looking up that song because it was always a balm for a hurt, a way to reinforce my belief that unwavering love was the golden chalice, or a way to justify the weight of the secrets I carried for others.

And it hit me.

I'd never sang that song to my own heart!

I'd sung it for others.

I longed to have it sung to me by anyone other than my mom.

I had never yet thought of singing this song to myself.

Tears were streaming down my face as I sang to my heart the promise I would never abandon it. The song continued to evolve as I later learned to hear the song being sung to me by the Divine. The Divine gifts of unconditional love, grace, forgiveness and acceptance washed over me as I imagined God standing over my body in that tub from the video. These values were the meat of the song that I craved. Steadfast consistent love and support. This wasn't only a ride or die anthem although it could be easily adopted and translated as such. It was the deep infinite love that could not be broken by circumstance.

Loyalty, while beautiful, should never come at the expense of self-care. True love requires balance, as well as a mutual exchange of support and understanding. And love, though unconditional in nature, doesn't translate to non-existent boundaries between people.

As I move forward, I strive to remember that standing by someone also means standing by myself. "I'll stand by you," I still promise, but now I include myself in that vow. Because in the end, the most profound loyalty we can offer is to our own heart. And it is more than loyalty. It is devotion.

I first heard this song in 1994 when it came out and, as I write this, it is 30 years old! I was 21 years old at the time and it was my theme song for love. I had no idea that I would hold the values of this song for almost two decades and that through these tough and loyal experiences of relating, I'd be forged into the energetic practitioner, mentor, and shadow worker that I am. I went on to create an Applied Energetic Philosophy rooted in conscious endings, impermanence, and presence. Literally, a practice of holding space for my own emotions and history as well as others without judgment. I still love in this way. It has woven its way into my entire being. Chrissie Hynde's strong yet tender voice, and the rustic romantic outlaw video that accompanied it, is one of the easiest recalls I have although the meaning of the song has changed quite a bit experientially for me. The nostalgia attached to the ideals and experiences that this song represented for decades is gone.

The Pretenders never had a successful single that topped this release. The song has also been redone by Girls Aloud, Carrie Underwood, and Shakira. Across the world, and time, it has stood out as a power ballad and specifically as a way to muster strength to be faithful through, and in, dark times.

I've never heard the song the same way again after I learned to create and uphold healthy boundaries. It is a much wider and deeper love song for me now. It shaped me in a real way. It shaped my philosophy and how I work with others in the long run. I had some very very intense and powerful love affairs that I assure you would not have been possible without the reassurance from this song! It validated some extremely poor choices on one hand and led me to the discovery of true unconditional love on the other. It touched my pain points deeply and offered relief in a testament of devoted, steadfast, non-judgmental love. Even though I'm no longer anybody's 'ride-or-die girl, this song has been my ride-or-die companion on an epic journey of self-discovery, heartbreak, and peace.

I also know now, I can't protect others from being hurt and I can't promise to shield the world from the bitterness and pain that coexists with bliss and beauty. This weight off my back feels great. My devotion to loving myself and the world unconditionally through daily practice stands firm. My empathy for others in pain is great. My resilience for hard love and darkness and confessions is great. And my heart, tender as it may be, has become a cherished compass I'll cradle in my best intentions till the day we both die.

Forever Young – Rod Stewart

Author: Michelle Wolfe

Some songs have a way of reaching into the past and pulling forth memories like pages from a well-loved book. "Forever Young" by Rod Stewart is one of those songs for me. Every time I hear it, I am transported—first, to my own childhood, where life felt simpler and full of possibility. And then to the present moment, where I stand as a parent, looking at my own children and hoping they never lose that boundless sense of wonder and freedom. This song carries a poignant nostalgia, a reminder of the passage of time and the delicate balance between growing up and holding onto the essence of youth.

I want to dedicate this chapter to my kids—to their bright futures, to their limitless potential, and to my deepest wish for them: to remain forever young at heart, and in spirit, and in the way they move through life.

When I was younger, the world felt vast and uncharted. There were no limitations, no barriers between me and my dreams. I remember the endless summer days, the kind that stretched on forever, when the sun felt warmer and the air smelled sweeter. Riding my bike with no particular destination, feet off the pedals, arms stretched wide like wings, I was weightless. The sound of cicadas filled the air, mingling with the distant laughter of children playing, the rhythmic squeak of a swing set, and the occasional hum of a song drifting from a nearby radio. Growing up in the '80s, "Forever Young" became part of the soundtrack of my childhood. When it comes on, I am immediately thrown back to that time—the sheer joy of movement, the wind in my hair, the unshakable belief that anything was possible.

Hearing "Forever Young" now, as an adult, evokes a bittersweet kind of nostalgia. It reminds me of those days of freedom and possibility, but also of how life has changed. The responsibilities of adulthood, the weight of expectations, and the way time seems to move so much faster now than it did when I was a child. Rod Stewart's lyrics feel like a promise— wishing sunshine, happiness, and protection over those we love, even when they're far from home. That line always feels like a blessing.

Becoming a parent shifts everything. Suddenly, your heart exists outside of you, in the form of the little people you've brought into this world. Every wish, every hope, every dream you ever had for yourself now extends to them. With a song like "Forever Young," I don't just hear it as a reflection of my own past—I hear it as a message to my children. It is my prayer for them, my blessing over their lives. I want them to hold onto their joy, to be courageous and brave, to see themselves as the powerful creators of their own stories. And when they leave the nest and fly away one day, all I can hope is that I've served them well—that I've loved and guided them in ways they'll carry forever.

Parenting is about guiding, about nurturing, about giving our children the tools to one day fly on their own. And when they do, we can only hope that we have given them the strength and wisdom to soar. I hope, one day, "Forever Young" will be a song that reminds them of me, of my love for them, and of all the moments we have shared together. I hope they think of the car rides when we laughed and sang at the top of our lungs, the nights we danced in the kitchen and had hysterical tickle fights, the quiet moments when I held them close and whispered how much they were loved. I hope they remember some of the freedom they felt as children—the sense that the world was theirs to explore—and that they carry that feeling with them always.

Music has an incredible way of shaping our identities, anchoring us to memories, and even influencing the way we see the world. "Forever Young" is more than just a song; it is a philosophy, a way of being. It's about living with an open heart, embracing life with courage, and holding onto the things that make us feel alive. For my children, I hope this song becomes part of their own personal soundtrack. I hope that when they hear it, they feel loved, even when they are far away, living their own lives separate from me. I hope they remember the lessons I try to teach them: that they are powerful, that they are worthy. That their perspective matters and adds to the tapestry of world views and perspectives available for us to come to know and understand ourselves better.

One of my greatest wishes for my children is that they never feel boxed in by the expectations of the world. I want them to know that they can dream as big as they want, that they can forge their own paths, and that they do not need to conform to anyone's version of success or happiness. The world will try to mold them, to tell them who they should be, but my hope is that they will always listen to their own inner voice first. That they will always remember the feeling of running barefoot through the grass, the magic of believing in something before the world told them it wasn't possible, the rush of swinging so high they felt like they might take off and touch the sky. That they will carry that feeling into adulthood, knowing they are only ever limited by their own sense of imagination.

One of the most beautiful things about music is its ability to connect generations. When I share meaningful songs with my children, I pass on a piece of myself, a piece of my past, and a piece of my deepest hopes. Music has a way of imprinting on our souls, becoming a part of our story.

To me, it's a reminder to live fully, to love deeply, and to embrace the magic of life. It is a call to remain curious, to take risks, and to never lose sight of what makes us feel alive. I take this song as an invitation. An opportunity to reconnect with my own youthful spirit, to remember that it is never too late to dream, to explore, to grow. I remind myself that the child who once believed anything was possible still exists within me — and that I can still connect with her at any time.

For my children, this is my wish: that they remain forever young. That they see the world with wonder, that they move through life with courage, and that they never forget how deeply they are loved. *I hope they remember that "whatever road they choose, I'm right behind them, win or lose."* And I send this wish out into the universe: "May good fortune be with you. May your guiding light be strong." May you always, in the ways that matter most, remain *forever young.*

Nothing Compares 2 U – Sinead O'Connor

Author: Melissa Rymer

I froze in my tracks, goosebumps rising on my skin, the first time I heard this song in 1990. It was the era of music videos, and the TV was tuned to *Rage*, a morning music show. I was making breakfast when Sinead's shortly cropped blonde hair and piercing hazel eyes stared straight down the barrel of the camera. As the lens zoomed in closer, it felt as if she was singing directly to me.

Her beauty was striking, otherworldly, but not in the serene, ethereal way of an angel. She looked more like a Buddhist monk—rageful and raw, her pain so palpable it was frightening. I wanted to look away but couldn't.

Her voice was a clarion call, her soul laid bare, longing for something vast and undefinable. I didn't fully understand it at the time, but her yearning struck a chord deep inside me, awakening my own unarticulated desires for a life and a love beyond what I had ever known.

Every time I heard it, I cried along with her.

When "Nothing Compares 2 U" came out, I was living in Melbourne with my boyfriend. On paper, we seemed like the perfect match: he was a doctor, I was finishing my architecture degree. But our relationship was more pretense than partnership. At just 21, I could sense that our bond lacked the authentic, vulnerable love that could withstand the inevitable challenges of life.

At the time, I was consumed by my studies. Long hours were spent crafting models, writing essays, and ambitiously filming a short film for my final project. My boyfriend supported me, in his way, but when it was all over, I felt a restless pull in another direction.

I announced that I wanted to go to New York to study film, to follow my passion. He thought it was a terrible idea, but despite his resistance, I packed my bags and left.

Looking back, I marvel at how I knew—without fully understanding why—that chasing my dreams would offer me a love far greater than anything he could give me.

At 15, I had my first taste of love with Jack. It was sweet and innocent, tinged with the thrill of discovery. I remember riding a bus with him on a summer day, heading to his family's beach house. He discreetly showed me a condom packet in his bag, and though I was nervous, I trusted him.

Jack was kind and gentle during our first encounter, but soon after, something changed. He became distant, more interested in beer and sports than in me. I pleaded with him to explain, desperate to understand, but he didn't have the words—or the will—to care.

The breakup shattered me. In the wreckage, I wondered if I had been too easy, if I had made a mistake in giving myself to him. Like many teenage girls, I internalized the blame, convinced that my desirability—or lack thereof—was the problem. In truth, it was never about me.

But I didn't know that then. I began a pattern of seeking out dangerous, unavailable men, confusing sex with love, and mistaking intensity for intimacy.

It took years, but my attitudes toward love and sex have evolved. Today, I approach relationships with a sense of agency I didn't know I needed. Desire, pleasure, intimacy, and love are beautiful when they align, but they are not essential. What is non-negotiable is self-love and care, mirrored in the connections I choose. Without that foundation, I know it isn't good for me—or my heart.

After a long and difficult 20-year partnership, during which I raised two sons, I met my lover. I was 52.

What began as an experiment to "take a lover" and help me transition out of the most harrowing period of my life blossomed into a tender and passionate love affair. For the first time, I found myself with a man who was kind, deeply appreciative, and open-hearted. His gentleness helped me heal ancient wounds, rewriting the story of abandonment that had haunted me since childhood.

Of course, the limerence—the heady cocktail of early love— eventually faded. But we were prepared for its passing. That was when the real work of love began: the hard conversations, the messy emotions, and the shared commitment to an authentic life.

As I approach 60, I find myself in a time of reckoning. I no longer have the luxury of wasting years worrying about whether I am lovable or worthy. The desire to lose myself in another has lost its allure.

Instead, I'm focused on loving myself with a depth I once reserved for others.

Now, when I listen to "Nothing Compares 2 U," I no longer hear it as a romantic love song. For me, its heartbreak and rage resound as a cry for help, a lamentation of enmeshment and codependency. The lyrics speak to the universal struggle of finding one's way in a complicated world, a world that often confuses possession with connection, longing with love.

When I learned of Sinead O'Connor's passing, I felt a profound sadness. She was a truth-teller, a visionary with an extraordinary gift, yet her courage often went unrecognized or was met with hostility. Like so many passionate and outspoken women before her, she was misunderstood, her brilliance overshadowed by a society that didn't know how to hold her intensity.

"Nothing Compares 2 U" will forever hold a fragment of her essence for me—a reminder of the bittersweet complexity of being human, a woman, and a mother in a messy and perplexing world.

"All the flowers that you planted, in the backyard, All died when you went away." – Lyrics by Prince

Rest in power, Sinead O'Connor (1966–2023).

Your Ex Lover is Dead - Stars

Author: Jeremy Nigli

"When there's nothing left to burn, you must set yourself on fire."

This was the era of Blackberries, unlimited incoming calls and paying per text. Passion Pit was playing that week. They weren't my fave, but Ellen really wanted to go, so I bought hard-copy tickets from Play de Record after school to save on fees. Doors were at 8, and the venue changed from the Phoenix to Kool Haus to accommodate an extra thousand people.

We were both students at the time, so money was tight. To save a few bucks, we ended up parking at Islington station and taking the TTC downtown. There was only one problem. At the last minute, Ellen changed her mind on the show. Since there wasn't much time to flip the tickets on craigslist, I agreed to help her sell them at the door, and we'd go out to dinner somewhere after with the money.

It was a cloudy day, and by the time we met at Union Station and started walking to the venue, it was already 7:30. Now known as the first place Drake ever performed in concert, Kool Haus was then in its heyday. It was one of several venues in The Guvernment, a larger complex renovated only two years prior. In 2008, the complex made the top ten of DJ Mag's top 100 clubs on the annual list at number 8 in the world. It was hot. Tonight was no different – Underworld was performing. Best known as the group behind the Trainspotting soundtrack, they were a rave throwback. Naturally, the crowd reflected that and made me, stone sober, uncomfortable. Oversized furry jackets, bracelets, glow sticks and the occasional pacifier joined us in our skinny jeans, band tees and American Apparel hoodies. As we got closer the skies darkened, and it began spitting.

I was always over-prepared, so I had a jacket. Ellen didn't. I did my gentlemanly duty and suggested she head somewhere so she could stay covered while I braved the crowds. She eagerly agreed, sauntering off to a bar down the street.

I kept going and stood near the main entrance on the east side, somewhat close to two dudes, each with a sign that said, "Need tickets." They were standing back-to-back. One was shorter and wore a red Roots poor boy cap from the '98 Olympics. It covered his bald head from the rain and stuck out because everything else he wore was drab and oversized. He had a scraggly goatee and moustache that signaled a lack of personal hygiene. The other dude was taller and irritated that his spiky gelled hair was getting wet. He had a three-stripe track jacket that was doing nothing to help him stay dry. His jeans were a bit too tight, and his Nike Shox had seen better days. He begrudgingly pulled out a grey beanie and put it on. They worked the crowd with predatory efficiency. Scalpers.

I wanted to offload the tickets, but I also wanted to get as much as I could for them. Playing the odds and hoping for the best, I approached Red Hat. "I have two tickets for Passion Pit." "Twenty bucks," he said.

I blinked, incredulously. The tickets cost $50 each, and that was the non-Ticketmaster price.

"Eighty," I countered.

He reached for the ticket, flashing a yellow-toothed grin with teeth that looked like half eaten popcorn.

"Forty," he said, pausing dramatically, "for both."

I yanked the ticket from his grasp, shaking my head as he snarled, "Fuck outta here." Determined to avoid further confrontation, I moved closer to the entrance and security.

The crowd was huge because both shows were being held at the same time. Plus, it had started to rain so everyone wanted to be inside. I passed a guy in a dark orange furry jacket. He smelled like camphor and onions and his pupils were saucers. He was smiling from ear to ear. Behind him were two young women, their band tees and hoodies clinging to them in the downpour. Their matching vans screamed emo. One was a brunette, and the other was blonde, and both were attractive. I overheard them say the word tickets. Crossing my fingers for luck, I decided to approach them.

"You guys going to Passion Pit?" The brunette looked at me skeptically. "You're not a scalper, are you?", she said. "Um, no. When's the last time a scalper hustled tickets below face value?" I asked. "I only want $80 for the pair." The blonde laughed as I continued to explain and shared that Ellen was at the bar down the street. The word "girlfriend" made all the difference. While the blonde's body language softened, her brunette friend crossed her arms, glancing at me with suspicion. "This better not be a scam," she warned. As if she couldn't tell the difference. "It's not," I said, showing them the hard-copy tickets. "I got these from Play de Record. No print-at-home nonsense."

Just as we were about to exchange funds, Red Hat materialized, flanked by his taller companion, Beanie. I hadn't noticed them double-timing in our direction because I was too focused on the girls. "Okay, $100 for both," Red Hat shouted. Brunette burst out laughing, then said, "How come you dropped your price all of a sudden?"

Wrong move.

Red Hat's face glared and his colour shifted to match his headwear. He shot daggers at me and snarled, "Fuck off dude, you got a problem?"

The crowd turned to look our way. The tension was unbearable. Suddenly, Red Hat shoved me hard. I stumbled backward, keeping a grip on the tickets. Beanie decided to join the fracas and echoed, "Yo, you got a problem?" while stepping aggressively in my direction. His right hand crossed his body, holding something awkwardly in his jacket.

Brunette said, "It doesn't matter to me who we get tickets from." That felt like a punch in the gut, given her role in the situation. Blonde's face had lost all colour.

I did the math: we were 10 feet from the entrance, and I knew the scalpers wouldn't come much closer. There were too many rent-a-cops, and the real deal prowled on the regular too.

Seizing my opportunity, I turned to the girls. "Let's get to the door. Once the tickets scan, you'll know they're real." Brunette looked at the massive line at the box office, shrugged and agreed. We ran straight to the security checkpoint.

The tickets scanned perfectly.

Blonde handed me the cash, and they both went inside. "Sorry," she said sheepishly. I forced a smile but was too stressed to respond. My immediate concern was how to leave without passing the scalpers again.

I texted Ellen and told her to get a cab as soon as possible. I didn't want to alarm her, but I knew the only exit was the way I'd come, and Red Hat and his partner were waiting. As

I surveyed my options, I struck up a conversation with a bouncer. He was well over six feet with arms the size of my legs and hair sprouting wherever it could find skin. He was fully dressed in black with an all-black Yankees cap, black Air Forces and a solitary gold chain. I noticed he had an accent and placed it correctly as Turkish.

We touched on the crazy crowds and the sudden switch in venue, and then Big Turk asked about me. I told him about Red Hat and Beanie. He got angry, puffed out his chest and said, "Let me take care of it for you." Big Turk called a security guard from another section and asked him to watch his post for a few minutes. He strolled confidently in the direction of the exit. I was stoked that if nothing else, the fight would be fair – two on two.

When he spotted the two men, he looked over his shoulder and back at the guard who replaced him. The other guard was vehemently shaking his head. Big Turk's face changed. He said gruffly, "I can't help you," then slowly turned his back to me and returned to his post. I followed behind. Now, how do I get out of here? Shocked and scared for my safety, I said, "Hey man, what happened?" He looked at me and said, "If you hurt them, more will come."

Crap. They're "connected."

My heart pounded as I considered my options. Big Turk pointed to a side exit through the neighboring building. I nodded thanks and slipped through the crowd, praying the two scalpers wouldn't see me. I was starting to panic because there was Ellen to consider as well. What if they hurt her? I moved as quickly as I could, ignoring the confused looks of the ravers around me as I elbowed past them. I ducked into the side street and slid out the south side of the building onto Lower Jarvis. I took a deep breath, hands on my knees, sweat bleeding through my hoodie. I let the butterflies in my stomach subside. I was safe.

I took a quick second to text Ellen and convey the urgency. I asked her to flag a cab from Richardson and Queens Quay. It was where all the cabbies parked and waited and was only a block over. I walked south on Lower Jarvis and turned right, heading towards Richardson, staring down at my phone in the hopes that I'd hear back.

Thwack! I got hit in my collarbone. The force of the impact snapped my head back.

I looked up. It was Beanie. He almost landed a sucker punch. Red Hat was right behind him, chuckling menacingly.

"Now, who's got a problem, mother-fucker?" he sneered. I could smell the alcohol on his breath.

Out of nowhere, the adrenaline hit and turned an already difficult situation into jittery chaos. I backed away, hands up, maintaining my stance while I did. "Look, man, I'm just a broke student," I said, my voice cracking, my throat dry.

"Fuck outta here, asshole," Red said as he lunged towards me with a kick that caught the outside of my shin. I took it well. Beanie's eyes registered surprise when he saw I hadn't dropped. I kept backing away, staying upright. I was about to pass a concrete doorway and knew if I got stuck there, I'd be curb-stomped.

My goal was to survive.

I was sweating so profusely that I felt like I hadn't worn a jacket. Even with the rain, I could feel the salt burning my eyes. I inched backwards while doing my best to stay out of striking distance of both Beanie and Red. I began to pray. This isn't how I wanted to go out. I looked around for anyone to help me, and the only things I could see were the orbs of the streetlamps, hazy in the downpour. I was alone.

I kept moving and realized I made it past the first doorway.

Success.

I was creeping towards Richardson Street.

Fuck.

There was another doorway - and this time, the light pole and parked cars boxed me in. There was nowhere to go. I saw a glint of metal where Beanie's hand was in his jacket, and my heart leapt to my throat.

Shit. I'm gonna die today.

Out of the corner of my eye I saw Ellen running toward us. It went scalpers, me, her. A shit sandwich.

I waved her back, terrified she'd get hurt. "HELP!" I screamed. "Call 911!"

Time was moving way too slowly for my liking.

Beanie closed in, his hand still in his jacket. Red Hat's fists were clenched, his movements erratic. Ellen was still, conspicuous in her silence.

Beanie moved towards the street to prevent me from running. I'm cooked, I thought. I'm going to have to fight. I figured I'd get at least one good shot in, and I knew it better be Beanie because I didn't want to find out what weapon I'd glimpsed earlier. I'd have to take my chances with Red Hat. He was bigger, but I was faster and sober.

Just then, the flashing red and blue lights of a police car pierced the darkness. The scalpers froze in place, and I pushed Ellen back, taking the opportunity to put some distance between them and us. The cops sped past. My heart sank – they weren't stopping.

Red began running towards us like an injured buffalo, and that's when the second police car peeled out from around the corner, its siren blaring. Beanie caught up to Red Hat and pulled him away. With Red Hat spitting profanities in my direction, they both disappeared into the night. Not taking anything for granted, I grabbed Ellen 's wrist and began running towards Richardson Street and our freedom. Just before we got there, Ellen shook my hand off and started waving. A cab emerged out of the mist, and I hopped in. At least that part of the night was easy. Ellen said, "Islington Station, please."

We had captured a taxi, despite all the rain.

The ride back to the subway was silent and tense. We didn't say a word. I was in shock. While rivulets flowed from the windshield onto the Gardiner Expressway, my eyes were waterless. I was still shaking. Ellen was unperturbed. We each had our own window, and the cracked leather between us may as well have been an ocean.

We finally made it back to Islington, where Ellen had parked her mid 90's Camry station wagon. So much for going out to dinner. My fists were still clenched, my chest tight with residual fear. The only thing Ellen had was damp hair and spots on her glasses. She opened the door to her car and I got in.

I asked the universe for a sign, as if I didn't already know that Ellen's Mp3/CD player was the only current item in a car held together by hopes and dreams. As Lupe Fiasco faded into The Stars and Todor Kobakov's string arrangements hit like a baroque Battle Hymn of the Republic - I knew.

Sometimes, no matter how much we care, things fall apart. Still, I'm not sorry. Not for meeting her, not for trying, not even for failing. I'm not sorry there was nothing to save - except myself.

I lived through it, and I won't look back.

November Rain – Guns N' Roses

Author: Michelle Wolfe

I was sitting at my ex-husband's kitchen table, a pile of new clothes between us, scissors in hand as we clipped tags off pants and shirts for the kids. The crinkle of plastic tags and the occasional snip of scissors filled the room. The mundane task grounded me, a necessary follow-up to the joyful chaos of our earlier family outing. We'd just spent the afternoon shopping together, the kids excitedly picking out fleece blankets and new outfits. It was one of those moments where I felt the warmth of co-parenting done right—easy camaraderie with my ex, a shared focus on the children we both love so fiercely.

But beneath that warmth was a heaviness I couldn't shake. **Heartbreak has a way of lingering, threading itself through even the simplest, happiest moments.**

Just a few months earlier, I had ended a relationship with someone I truly believed could be my forever person. The weight of that loss pressed down on me, even as I tried to lose myself in the rhythm of the scissors and the joy of the day. Pandora playing classic rock tunes in the background. And then, as if on cue, "November Rain" by Guns N' Roses came on.

Suddenly, I was no longer in that kitchen. The song carried me back to 14-year-old me, sitting in the back seat of my mom's Ford Taurus on the way to Ocean City, Maryland. My Walkman CD player hummed in my lap as I gazed out the window, lost in the swelling emotions of teenage dreams and heartbreaks I hadn't yet experienced but somehow already felt.

And now here I was, 42 years old, just months out of a breakup with a man I had truly opened my heart to. Someone I thought might be somebody for me. And he was, but not in the ways I saw for us. Sitting at the table, scissors poised over a price tag, I stopped mid-cut. The familiar melody and Axl's mournful lyrical poetry seemed to echo my own heartache. My ex-husband looked up, noticing my stillness.

"It's crazy how you can listen to a song so many times but suddenly it hits differently, isn't it?" I said, tears welling in my eyes. I looked away, letting the lyrics wash over me.

It's funny how a song can change like that for you over time. When I was a teenager, "November Rain" was just a beautiful, dramatic ballad, full of longing and melancholy that I couldn't yet grasp. At 14, the song felt distant, like a story that belonged to someone else. But in that moment, sitting at that kitchen table, it catapulted me into a surreal moment of realization. I had lived through the kind of heartbreak it described—the aching disconnect of loving someone who struggled to meet me. That's what caught me, stopping me in my tracks. I could suddenly relate to the song's mournful yearning, its quiet acceptance of inevitable loss, and the way it captured the fragility of love with someone who keeps themselves just out of reach.

It wasn't just a song anymore—it was a reflection of my experience, and it felt deeply, almost painfully, personal.

The part where the song builds – the crescendo of emotion – drops, and I told Alexa to turn it up, and my ex-husband and I sat in silence, absorbing the raw beauty of that moment. Slash's musical genius tore through the air, and for a brief moment, time stood still.

Sitting there with my ex, clipping tags and mending the pieces of my broken heart, I felt an overwhelming gratitude. Gratitude for the way life evolves, for the space to process where I was and how far I'd come.

The man I dated after my divorce felt like he was going to be my person. He felt like a match in so many ways and there was this mystical energy between us; an almost otherworldly fated type of connection. Maybe because we both love dragons, mythical creatures, dark arts and have a shared fascination for life in mutually stimulating ways. We shared beautiful moments of intimacy and connection. I am truly grateful for what we shared and the safety I experienced just being myself with him. His warmth and the comfort I felt in his arms, after having dissolved a marriage and stepping out on my own for the first time in almost two decades, is something that will stay with me.

I learned powerful truths in the aftermath. First and foremost: slow the fuck down. I had been ready to choose him forever after the first date. While I believe in feeling instantly at home with someone, I now know that allowing the bond to grow slowly over time is essential to truly understanding someone's soul. In hindsight, I didn't really know him, even though I'd *known of* him for 15 years. I just felt so at ease with him.

But his hesitance was always there. I could sense it, even when he denied it. He valued his freedom and autonomy, and while I honored that and even found those aspects of him attractive, it clashed with my need for connection, consistency, and affection.

That relationship forced me to face the parts of myself I didn't want to see—the messy, broken, dark corners I tried to hide even from myself. It was in that space that I started healing my attachment wounds, my codependency, and the patterns of over-giving and self-abandonment I had carried since childhood.

When I realized the writing was on the wall, I stopped trying to repair us and began to repair myself.

I journaled endlessly, trying to untangle the knot of emotions. I battled with myself, wanting to let go but unable to fully release him. "Everybody needs some time on their own – all alone," the song reminded me. And in that time alone, I found myself. I poured my energy into my passion projects, like this book, and into healing the parts of me that had been hurting for so long. I sat in self-reflection and rebuilt my sense of self. Slowly, I began to see the breakup not as a loss, but as a catalyst for growth.

Looking back, I see it clearly now. I am an expansive, emotionally attuned woman on a perpetual growth journey. I have lofty goals, a soul purpose to fulfill, and an audacity to want to create meaningful contributions to the world. I need a partner who can meet me there, who wants to walk this path with me. The relationship had been a mirror, showing me parts of myself I needed to confront.

I always sensed he was purposely holding back. Withholding affection, expression, love—even though deep down I think he felt it and I certainly felt it emanating off of him. He seemed to be self-protective, guarded. And, in response, I guarded myself from him. Instead of chasing, convincing, and wanting him to choose me—I chose myself and ultimately let him go. I chose to honor my needs and walk away from a connection that didn't align with the love I deserve.

Being with him undoubtedly made me a better person. I appreciate how he invited me to explore my edges. He helped me embrace more joy and laughter, face my shadow with courage, and step into a more empowered version of myself. But he also showed me what I don't want—a relationship riddled with breadcrumbs, confusion, deprivation, and hesitation. This man evoked so much in me. He inspired me. Not because of anything he did outright, though I witnessed him in some beautiful human moments that made me feel awe. In some cases, it was what he didn't do that motivated me to step into a better version of Self.

Listening to "November Rain" now, I can see how that relationship showed me the parts of myself that still needed healing and helped me solidify my relationship with my inner child. And though the pain of letting go was immense, it gave me the strength to love myself more fully. I honor his need for freedom while also acknowledging my own need for reciprocal love and partnership that is present.

It was hard to draw that line. I knew I'd miss him, and us, once it was done. But if I've learned anything it's that these hard moments don't last forever. The pain of letting go will fade and new adventures await. I've gotten more adept at being my own best friend and I genuinely enjoy spending time by myself. That is my creative time, my reflective time, and where I find myself again and again.

Sometimes I think about him and his hyper-independence and his refusal to rely on others for support and I wonder if he'll ever let that guard down.

"Everybody needs somebody...you're not the only one."

But from now on, anytime I hear this song... a song that has been with me since I was a tween-teen... I will think of him and smile.

Because that's the thing about rain—it doesn't last, but the growth it brings does.

You Get What You Give – New Radicals

Author: Jennifer Eggerts

The lyrics to this song have played on my heart and soul for 25 years. They have been a beacon of hope and have become an almost battle cry for my growth and recovery. The first time I heard the song "You Get What You Give," I was in my car driving on HWY 101 in Santa Barbara. I pulled over before the song was over because I was in tears. There I was, driving around in paradise and yet I was miserable. I was 18 years old and completely lost at sea.

The song *saw* me...

It saw my hope...

My fear...

My anger...

My passion...

...and I needed all those parts seen and validated at that time in my life.

The song itself came out in 1998 when I was a freshman at the University of California, Santa Barbara. I was not at all prepared to be away from home and had tried desperately to "self-sabotage" my way out of a four-year university by failing AP Chemistry. It did not work. I ended up taking summer school and still getting into 80% of the colleges in which I applied.

Though I was nervous about the academic load of my freshman year, it ended up being manageable. While I handled the academic component easily, I regularly felt isolated from my peers. I am an introvert and neurodivergent. I didn't like partying and I really just wanted to go home.

I was headfirst into a gnarly battle with a serious eating disorder before winter break. My plan was simple. Starve as hard as I could until someone noticed and intervened. I channeled every hope and fear into perfecting my eating disorder. I was angry, disillusioned and like a fish out of water.

The lyrics were like balm to my soul. I had no idea how I was going to "fix myself" and listening to the song gave me hope that I could get better. I played it quite a bit the year it came out. By the final quarter of my freshman year, I was incredibly underweight and no longer able to focus on my studies.

My life had become consumed with calorie counts, exercise, and an obsession with perfection. My eating disorder became my identity and keeping it a secret was time consuming. Not coincidentally and at about this same time, I was discovering just how sensitive and perceptive I was as well. I just "knew stuff" about people and about life that were both way beyond my years and very often, incredibly insightful. I was tortured by my inability to regulate my own emotions, let alone be able to recognize the difference between my emotions and another's.

The irony did not escape me even then:

I was starving my light while listening to a song about holding onto my light.

For the next 15 years, my life was a series of poor choices and addiction. Despite two major treatment interventions at 18 and 21, my eating disorder only stayed in remission until my late twenties. I spent over eighteen months in treatment.

I learned so much about myself in those years. I learned that I was highly intelligent and empathic. I learned that this particular combination was not easy to regulate and that I would have to balance the extremes of my nature for the rest of my life.

There is a line in this song that talks about bending. Oh, how I used to recite this as a mantra. Just bend. Just bend, Jen. How hard could it be, right?

I was ashamed of my mistakes. I felt like damaged goods, and by the time I graduated from undergrad I was on a mission to make up for the harm I had caused my family. I was going to redeem myself for my errors if it killed me.

The song became a way to motivate myself to hang on, by any means necessary. After graduating, I started working in education; primarily in a sales function. I was running an entire learning center by age 25 and it was the fourth largest center in the state. For a short time, I handled the stress and pressure well.

Until I didn't.

Remember when I said anorexia wasn't my only addiction? I come from a long line of addicts and alcoholics. I knew the dangers of alcohol, yet I started drinking with regularity. I was horrified by my behavior, yet it was the only way I could get my anxiety down enough to sleep at night. Before I knew it, I was drinking a bottle of wine a night and skipping dinner.

I was so unhappy and I honestly didn't understand why. I had everything I said I wanted – the job, the apartment, the boyfriend. I had it and I was miserable. I had it and my anxiety was through the roof. I had it and I was a starving drunk. I had it and I was empty.

I heard the song quite often in my late twenties and early thirties. Every time it came on the radio, I would change it as soon as it came on. It reminded me of how disconnected I was from myself or my music. It broke my heart because I was doing the best that I could and I was failing. Those days were so rough. The alcohol left me numbed out and hungover. The lack of food kept me malnourished and unable to think straight. I was locked out and locked in at the same time.

What I was doing had an expiration date. It turned out, that end date was 12/21/12. I don't remember much from that day. Even now, it's still fuzzy and I'm unsure of whether it's real memory or some patch work of stories recounted to me and echoes of trauma. That morning I felt very odd upon waking. As my feet hit the floor, my knees buckled under my weight as I was overcome by dizziness and nausea. Something was very wrong. I could not think straight and I was terrified. Somehow I managed to get myself to an urgent care facility on foot. They transported me to the ER and called my parents.

That day, and the days that followed, were a blur. I'd had what was akin to a small stroke and I was lucky to be alive. Between the heavy alcohol intake and almost no food, my body was ridiculously unhealthy. It was clear that I needed more help. And I was ready and I was willing.

I spent the next ten months unraveling the previous fifteen years of poor choices, trauma information, depression and anxiety. It was not at all like my treatment experiences as a younger woman. It was harder, scarier, and felt so much more hopeless. It was two addictions rather than just one. I had to meet the worst parts of myself on repeat every day.

This was also where I met myself for the first time. So many of the messages that I carried about myself were inaccurate and served only to reinforce my addictions. As I stepped away from the version of me that needed to "fix" negative emotion I began to realize that the emotions themselves were not nearly as scary as I believed them to be, nor did sitting with them until they passed hurt as much as I thought it would.

In the chorus of this song, it talks about the music living inside of you. While it was something I knew about myself cognitively, it took me well into the fifth year of my sobriety to actually believe that my music was something worth hearing or sharing. As I became more willing to listen to my hopes and dreams, I began to realize that the life I thought I wanted was less about me and more about conditioning. Some of the conditioning was ancestral, some societal and some was of my own making.

I wish I could say that my awareness alone gave me the ability to step away from struggle, strife and suffering. It did not, and at times I still find myself in all three of these states. The last six months have been some of the most difficult of my life. What has changed about these states for me, however, is how I relate to myself and how I forge ahead inside of them.

My life today is less about external achievement and more about internal states of being. Today I work diligently to cultivate a compassionate yet accountable relationship with myself. This involves repeatedly asking myself what I want, what I can achieve without throwing myself into depletion and what are the most pragmatic ways to go about getting where I want to go. I experiment quite frequently and, while I do not like falling on my face, I have developed a certain sense of humor about being a work in progress.

I don't require my best in any situation anymore, nor do I allow myself to sit in paralysis either. This is how I learned to "get" what I "gave."

For so long I was unsure of how to extend my gifts back to myself. I am so motivated by service, and I am truly at my best when my focus is on something greater than just myself or my healing. It was only when I regularly started practicing being of service to my highest self that I felt the love I was sharing with others. Even now there are still times that I really struggle to be kind to myself. It is a practice and today, it is one I look forward to evolving.

My hope is that in the coming years, the efforts I have made really start to influence my life in positive ways. I have learned to bend with grace more often and with greater ease. My intuitive sense tells me that they will and the fact that I'm still here is a testament to my grit and tenacity.

Time After Time – Cyndi Lauper

Author: Michelle Wolfe

A song that has followed me through life, hitting differently each time… *time after time.*

Music has a way of embedding itself into the fabric of a life. Certain songs become more than just melodies or lyrics; they become timestamps, woven into the moments that matter, into the people who leave imprints on the heart. "Time After Time" is one of those songs for me. It has followed me like a gentle echo, appearing at the right times, carrying a message I can't always articulate but always feel.

It's hard to say which version is my favorite. There have been many interpretations, each bringing something unique— different textures, different emotions—but I always find myself coming back to Cyndi Lauper's version. Perhaps because it's the most well-known. Perhaps because it still, without fail, makes me pause, makes me *feel*. It softens me in whatever I'm doing, like a flutter in the chest, a quiet but persistent nudge from the universe. If you know, you know.

There is something mystical about this song, a subtle magic in the way it appears, often when least expected but most needed. It's not that every time it plays, I drop everything and search for meaning. I love music, plain and simple. I can enjoy a song without overanalyzing it. But then there are the moments when a song refuses to be background noise. Some songs demand attention, refuse to be ignored. "Time After Time" is one of those songs for me.

I had one of those moments recently, sitting outside on a warm, sticky, end-of-summer night. The kind of night that lingers, that stretches time in a way only late summer evenings can. I was on a date—not just any date, but one of those firsts, where everything is still unfolding. The kind of night that feels like discovery, like stepping cautiously into new territory while carrying all the weight of the past.

It was the night I told him.

Not everything, of course. Not a full inventory of every mistake, every regret, every version of myself that had led me to that moment. But enough. Enough that he could see the parts of me I had once been ashamed of. Enough that he could decide if I was too much, if I was too complicated, if my past disqualified me from whatever possibility we were tiptoeing toward.

Divorced. A mother of two. A past filled with choices that hadn't always been right. I laid them out, not as a confession but as a way of saying: This is me. This is the road I've walked. Are you sure you want to take a step closer?

And he listened.

He listened as I judged myself more harshly than he ever could. He listened as I picked apart my own history, finding all the ways I could have been better, done better. He listened without flinching, without looking for an escape. And instead of agreeing with my worst fears, he challenged them. Played devil's advocate to my self-criticism. Interrupted my catastrophizing with a steadiness that unsettled me. He never once made me feel like I was anything less than human.

We sat there, holding hands across the table, the city buzzing around us but somehow, in that moment, it was just us. There was a lightness in the air, a contrast to the weight of the conversation. And then, from the speakers overhead, "Time After Time" began to play.

I noticed it, registered it in the background. But then, as the song came to an end, it started again.

And then, a third time.

Some things won't be ignored.

I don't believe in coincidences the way I used to. Maybe I never did. Maybe I've always felt there was something more, something unseen, guiding moments like these. The repetition of that song—on *that* night, in *that* conversation, with *that* person—felt like a whisper from something greater than me.

There are only a handful of people in life for whom this song truly applies. The kind of people who could get lost, wander far from themselves, and still know, if you fall, I will catch you. I will be waiting. That kind of love, that kind of connection, is rare. It doesn't bind, doesn't cage. It allows space. It says: *Go, explore, make mistakes, disappear if you need to… but if ever you need to find your way back, you know where I'll be.*

This song feels like a reflection of how I love. The way I show up for people. The way I anchor them when they feel untethered. There is devotion in it, yes, but also freedom. A knowing that love, real love, does not demand. It simply is. And maybe that's why this song feels so deeply intertwined with my relationship with this man.

We have always had a way of finding each other, time after time. Even in the space between us, even in the moments where silence stretches too long or fear takes hold, there is a thread that remains unbroken. The push and pull, the quiet knowing, the undeniable truth that something about us is different.

There is no need for constant closeness. If there were, we wouldn't have lasted. What exists between us is something else entirely. Something that allows for distance, for retreat, for solitude. Something that trusts the return.

And I suppose that's why this song has become a kind of anthem for me—not just in love, but in life. It is part of my mission here. To be the person who does not abandon so easily. To be the one who reminds others, in their darkest moments, that they are not alone.

That does not mean I stay in places that are unhealthy, or abandon myself to keep someone else close. I've had to release relationships—people I love deeply—because staying would have cost me too much. "What is this costing me?" on repeat in my mind. It's a dance of connection and boundaries.

I know what it's like to feel untethered. To wonder if anyone would notice if the ground beneath you disappeared. And maybe that's why I feel called to be this for others—an anchor, a reminder, a safe place to land.

And so, "Time After Time" remains. A song that has followed me, a song that carries layers of meaning that deepen with time. A song that reminds me that love, in its truest form, is something that does not demand, does not chase, does not force. It simply waits. It allows. It releases.

Time after time.

With You I'm Born Again – Billy Preston and Syreeta Wright

Author: Mariyam Hasham

How many times have I been in love?

It felt like a valid question at eighteen, even though I was too young to have a real past. I was still the girl from a Benedictine convent school—too polite, too good at keeping secrets. But that summer, everything changed.

It was the summer of warm Carolina sunshine and my first car, a summer of discovery, baseball games, and salsa classes. It was the summer that transformed me from a girl into a woman. And it was the summer I first heard Billy Preston and Syreeta Wright's "With You I'm Born Again" playing on the radio of a second-hand pickup truck on a Carolina beach.

I don't know what it was about Johnny D, but I fell in love with him the moment I saw him. His hair was too long, and so was his shirt. His eyes were dark indoors but turned a golden brown, shot through with amber, in the sunlight. A Carolina boy with Cuban parents, he drove a burnt umber pickup truck with oversized wheels—a trend in the South where boys raced each other on dirt tracks, chasing dreams with no money to make them happen.

Our first date was at McDonald's, the next at Dunkin' Donuts. We drank black coffee and ate slowly, trying to stretch our time together into infinity. He talked about cars, baseball, and the life he wanted someday, and I could've listened forever. His family was warm, loud, and full of life— a world apart from mine, where silence and slammed doors reigned.

His sisters taught me to dance salsa in their backyard under the moonlight, music spilling out of a crackling radio. Their vibrant energy and rhythm made me long to be like them. I grew to love Cuban music that summer, and with it, I began to understand the power of joy and connection in ways I never had before.

Music was something I didn't have much of before Johnny. My upbringing had been cold and rigid. Music was seen as frivolous at best, sinful at worst. The sultry warmth of salsa would have earned me years of penance in the convent school. Dancing with a boy—or even his father—was unthinkable. But that summer, I left all that behind.

On weekends, Johnny would drive us to Myrtle Beach. We'd lie on the sand, the radio playing softly in the background. Those golden days felt endless, and his heartbeat became the soundtrack of my life.

One night, while we lay too hot to touch under the Carolina stars, "With You I'm Born Again" played on the radio. Its lyrics spoke what I didn't have the words to say:

"*Come give me your strength. Now there is you, there is no weakness.*"

But summers end, and so do first loves. My path took me far from the USA to a graduate program in London, where I studied political violence and terrorist groups. My world became one of geopolitics, negotiations, and men who only saw me as an obstacle or an asset to exploit. I learned to navigate their hostility by becoming invisible. Silence became my superpower. I modeled myself after the coldest, most untouchable figures I could find — Russian mercenaries, fictional snow queens — learning to project an aura of detachment and control.

"I'm fine."
"I don't need anyone."
"It's cool. I've got this."

No FBI profiler could've cracked me. But underneath the armor, I couldn't forget the music that had softened my heart all those years ago.

For years, I avoided "With You I'm Born Again." I turned to jazz, Korean pop, Earth, Wind & Fire, Otis Redding, and Springsteen's early work. Music became a backdrop, a way to cope with London's cold winters. Eventually, I returned to salsa, renewing my love for the rhythms that had first opened me up.

Then one day, while preparing to interview a paramilitary prisoner, the song found me again. It surfaced unexpectedly, playing on YouTube as I reviewed my questions. It stirred something inside me—a faint memory of the girl I had been before I became untrusting and hypervigilant.

During the interview, I replayed the song in my head. I looked at the violent man sitting across from me and, for a moment, saw a 14-year-old boy with no friends, lingering on darkened streets because his home was cold and unsafe. I saw him when his heart was still open, and it changed the way I wanted to be.

I didn't absolve him of his violence or the terrible consequences of his actions. But I saw him as a wounded child navigating a broken world, his inner life shattered into fragments that exploded outward. And I didn't want to do him any more harm.

After that, I listened to the song before every interview. It became a way to shift my perspective, to see past hostility into the vast loneliness behind it. I didn't excuse their actions, but I saw their pain. I saw the humanity that violence had buried beneath years of loss and anger.

I still listen to "With You I'm Born Again." I listen for the woman I am now and the one I might yet become. I listen for Johnny D, for the men I met who will never again drink coffee with a girl or feel the warmth of a friend's laughter.

I listen for the strangers on the street whose lonely eyes I recognize, even in passing.

The right song connects us to who we are and who we've been. It allows us to soften in a world that demands hardness. It transforms us into invitations instead of demands, into calm breezes instead of storms.

Music is a balm, one we can always share, no matter how hard the road seems.

Do You Wanna Make Love – Peter McCann

Author: Louis Cinquino

Making love?!

As in…the love that makes the world go round? That crazy little thing you can't help falling into? What the world needs now?

Love, the drug that I'm thinking of?!

Yes. That is exactly what I wanted to make. Not macramé, not pet rocks, not model airplanes. I was a fifteen-year-old altar boy in the late 1970s, and what I wanted to make was love.

Also, I had no idea what that meant, or who to ask for clarification.

My friends were even more clueless than I was. My very Catholic parents certainly weren't going to help. My Golden Home and High School Encyclopedia had no entry for this matter. Lots of newspapers and a whopping three channels of TV—nothing. The only social media at the time were hand-me-down Playboys that were heavy on objects of desire but presumably light on the emotional complexities of relationships. (I did not read the articles.)

For that advice I would turn to my AM/FM clock radio and trusty cassette tape recorder. With the help of Casey Kasem's Top 40 countdown, I pieced together the lyrical wisdom of the supposed sages of love that filled the airwaves—and my impressionable mind.

It started off on the wrong foot with Badfinger.

"Day After Day" (1971) told me that key moment for a boy was apparently to just "find out" about a girl. The rest was easy. Like Columbus setting out for the New World, I just had to "discover" a girl, and she'd fall for me like I was a conquistador.

"Looking out from my lonely room, day after day."

Even better. No voyage necessary. I can just stay in my faux-wood paneled room, fantasize, and she will come to me. The song goes on to describe the peak romantic moment: holding her while she sleeps.

This is getting better and better – I don't even have to face my biggest fear: what to say to her.

My crucifix hung over my head as I took notes:

- All that matters is how I feel, not her
- Keep all emotions to myself, no talking necessary
- The more I go inward, the more she'll dig me

In other words, the perfect love song for a nine-year-old boy to sing to himself until he was ready to really find out what love is.

Badfinger's "Lonely Room" strategy worked well enough— until puberty hit.

By the time Kenny Nolan's "I Like Dreamin'" (1977) came along, I was a JV basketball player with a cheerleader crush and a plan.

She sat near me on the team bus. Her friend said she liked me and would go out with me. Kenny's advice mirrored Badfinger's so I was sure that asking her out was all I needed to do, which I did. She said yes! The rest would simply fall into place...

"I like dreamin' cause dreamin' can make you mine."

Perfect! I was already dreaming about her, so certainly she would soon be in my possession. Which meant, as the song went on, that (even though we lived in the snow belt near Buffalo) soon we'd be holding hands walking barefoot on the beach. If only!

And Kenny kept going. He sees our children's warm little smiles looking up at us. Wow. Okay. This is moving pretty fast, but YES, LET'S MAKE BABIES.

Dreamin' made her mine! With one small problem. As the song ends, the guy wakes up and she's ... just. not. there.

Wait, what? Not there?!

Sadly, Kenny was at least half-right, she was not there. After a month of "going out" and me being too nervous to actually go on a date or kiss, my first girlfriend turned into the first person to break up with me.

Shockingly, just dreaming about her was not enough to keep her happy. Kenny, what went wrong?!

My first time would have to wait. For that I would need more tangible, practical advice. I turned to Foreigner. Luckily, in "Feels Like the First Time" (1977), they gave me a clear set of instructions.

1. Climb any mountain.
2. Sail across the stormy sea.
3. Show how much she means to you.
4. Bring out the man in you.
5. Don't worry about what that actually means, because it's the woman in her that brings out the man in you.
6. Wait a lifetime.
7. Spend your time so foolishly.
8. Find HER.
9. Make history.

At least Foreigner was getting me out of my room. But such a high expectation – and an undue burden on this mythical first person to be MY treasure, MY personal savior, MY Niña, Pinta, and Mount Rainier all wrapped in one.

This quest also proved fruitless. Even 15-year-old me could see I needed a new approach beyond the four walls and fantastical journeys of my boyhood imagination to something even more daring and unimaginable than crossing a windswept ocean. I had to actually, honestly, talk to girls. Maybe even *with* them, openly, earnestly, from my heart.

Enter Peter McCann, who gave me the line I needed to interrogate my prospects, er, talk to girls. It seemed like progress, yet no song scarred me more than his "Do You Wanna Make Love" (1977). Its sensitive man mantra of boy-splaining and slut-shaming sent me careening into a confusing early adulthood of just not getting it- literally, figuratively, or otherwise.

"Do you wanna make love, or do you just wanna fool around?"

Step right up ladies, my obsession with you is the answer to your every desire. I don't need to keep it a secret anymore. I want to love you, L-O-V-E looooove you. No foolin' around!

All this (picture me standing in front of my full-length mirror, flexing suggestively) can be yours at a moment's notice. Before curfew! Why are you hesitating?

In the emotional peak of the song, McCann issues the ultimate threat, either take it seriously or take it somewhere else.

That seemed very far-fetched to me. I mean come on, could any self-respecting girl actually walk away in full knowledge of the love I've been keeping a secret for so long? To give up the chance for a real-life Love Story and just go fool around with some other guy who couldn't possibly love her more than I did?

And yet, when he looks in her eyes, he can't tell if it's love or … just. another. empty. lie.

This can't be happening. I finally get the nerve to announce my love to the world and you aren't boarding my Love Boat? I realize we just met. But you smiled at me! Are you nothing more than a shallow, stuck up, short-sighted silly girl deceiving me??

By now you have guessed that I did not make love that summer, or even fool around. It would take many years of unraveling the twisted logic of these so-called love songs to really discover what it meant to connect emotionally with a woman in a way that was meaningful to both of us.

The real-life lessons I learned in the relationships of my young adulthood came at a much higher price than those I suffered from the naivete of Seventies lyrics.

There were a couple legit girlfriends who stumbled through it with me in my heavy drinking days after college. They drank even more than I did, so we couldn't help each other, and those relationships sank in mutually assured destruction.

From those shipwrecks, I did salvage enough relationship competency to get married, but the stability of 21 years of marriage lulled me into thinking I didn't need to keep learning about myself and what intimacy really meant. It would take a painful divorce to shake that complacency out of me, sending me back into a different lonely room; that of unexpected bachelorhood.

At 50, my teenage dreams of walking on the beach were replaced with nightmares of what tsunamis lay ahead for me. Time to get out there again, now without Peter Effing McCann's sanctimonious mentoring.

So, the song went on. Every false start and breakup brought more lessons – and often more pain to me and my partners. Although this time it was in sobriety, so the lessons were easier to understand, even if they were still difficult to implement.

I did get better at talking, a byproduct of going on about 100 (dead end) first dates from the apps, seeing four therapists (and dating five more). I did not just stay in my room and expect Spotify to provide the answers.

I went through dozens of courses, seminars, tantra training, a positive psychology certificate, and countless books and podcasts. I sought out lectures, retreats, pilgrimages, spiritual practices, astrology, love languages, cold plunges, poetry, even circus school and psychedelics.

With each new attempt, I took one small step further from the boy steeped in possessive, lovelorn lyrical fantasies and nudged closer to becoming a man unafraid (ok, less afraid) of intimacy.

With apologies to Badfinger and the rest of those bands who I played repeatedly on my cassette player, I slowly grasped what they didn't tell me: that understanding my own patterns and peeling away my facades came first. And that holding space in safety and consent, listening with deep curiosity, and seeking mutual trust are more important in finding, protecting and making love (or just foolin around) than any stanza or repeating chorus can provide.

The buttons I push now are not Play. Stop. Rewind.

They are Pause. Listen. Share.

Down Bad – Taylor Swift

Author: Michelle Wolfe

Fuck you for all the ways you ruined what we could have been.

Fuck you for learning the things I loved
and withholding them from me.

Deprivation twisted up with Devotion.
This hurt dance that we do.

Where is it that you disappear to?
When you go away.
~ Michelle Wolfe

Oh, teenage angst. The kind that crashes into your chest and lingers, heavy and unrelenting. The kind that whispers heartbreak in every corner of your mind. And then there's "Down Bad"—a song so achingly raw, it felt like holding hands with the saddest parts of myself, singing a duet with my inner teenager.

The first time I played it, I was sitting on the floor next to my bed, knees drawn to my chest, the moonlight spilling across the room in jagged lines.

Taylor's voice slipped into the silence like a friend you didn't know you needed. When she sang, *"fuck it I was in love – so fuck you if I can't have us"* so softly, it wasn't just a lyric—it was a lifeline. There's something about Taylor Swift's music that makes you feel seen, even when you don't want to be. Her gentle defiance echoed in me, allowing me to let the storm of hurt move through me instead of pretending it wasn't there. It felt like a paradox, her voice soft enough to hold me, her words sharp enough to rip me apart.

I remember those first weeks after its release, how I played it on repeat like a ritual while I drove aimlessly through back roads. The weight of this heartbreak sat heavy in my chest. It became the backdrop to long drives with no destination, the soundtrack to staring out the window at summer rain tracing ghostly paths on the glass doors leading to my back balcony. That song wasn't just music—it was a mirror. It reflected all the anguish, disappointment, and rage I had been carrying, especially for the part of me that had wanted so much more and didn't get it.

When I think back to that time, I see the younger version of me was mourning—my inner teenager, who believed in forever love. The dreamer, the romantic, the girl who clung to the idea of her *"forever person."* She felt so deeply, hoped so fiercely, and wanted so much. But life had other plans. That version of me burning away in an alchemical fire, one I didn't know how to stop. Taylor's voice held me as I watched that part of myself dissolve into ash, whispering truths I wasn't ready to say out loud.

I wasn't a huge Taylor Swift fan until a few years ago. My son teases me endlessly now. *"Mom, you're such a Swiftie,"* he says, rolling his eyes, while my daughter nods in agreement, proudly adding Taylor's songs to her own playlists. I smile at their teasing because they don't know the half of it. They don't know how much her music has held me, shaped me, healed me. How she's given voice to the unspoken parts of my heart in ways I didn't expect.

It's not just the music; it's her courage, her relentless authenticity. You can hear it in every note, feel it in every lyric. Taylor is one of those artists who cracks herself open and invites you to do the same. She reminds me of Lady Gaga and other artists who live in that bold, vulnerable space of creativity. That's what makes them magnetic—the way they dare you to face yourself.

What I love about "Down Bad" is how it embraces that teenage angst and heartbreak without apology. It's not trying to sugarcoat the messiness of it all. It's real. And when I listen to it now, months later, I can still feel the echo of anguish, but it no longer belongs to me. The feelings have dulled, faded like the colors of an old photograph. It's like holding someone else's grief in my hands, tenderly, knowing it's a part of who I was but not who I am anymore.

Back then, though, I couldn't stop listening. Every repeat of the song felt like pouring salt into a wound, but I needed it. Music has a way of letting you stew in your pain, sit with it, almost befriend it. It gives you permission to feel everything you're trying to avoid. Songs like Duran Duran's "Come Undone" and 311's "Love Song" have always done that for me, pulling me into emotions I thought I'd left behind. And Taylor's "Down Bad" became part of that lineage—a song that reminded me of all the heartbreaks that had shaped me.

But this wasn't just a breakup song; it was a portal. A song that led me through the grief of losing not only someone I loved but the fantasies I had built around them. It showed me how much of my pain came from trying to hold onto control when all I could do was let go.

Letting go wasn't just about the relationship—it was about surrendering my idea of what love and partnership should look like. That teenage girl who dreamed of her "forever person" had to step aside for the woman I've become. Love isn't about finding someone to complete you; it's about choosing someone to dance with in life's great cosmic sandbox. And sometimes, the hardest choice is walking away from the dance when it stops serving you.

"Down Bad" also made me confront the parts of myself I didn't want to see—the messy, broken, dark corners I tried to hide even from myself. It forced me to acknowledge the ways I had clung to unhealthy patterns, letting go of codependency and beginning the hard work of healing my attachment wounds. Those relationships that cut you the deepest also have the power to transform you. If you let them. And that's what this song reminds me of now—not just the heartbreak but the healing. Not just the loss but the transformation.

Listening to it now is like opening a time capsule and finding the girl I used to be—disappointed, angsty, but still brave enough to hope. She may have been heartbroken, but she never gave up on herself. And maybe that's why I'll always love this song, no matter how far away those feelings feel. Because "Down Bad" wasn't just a soundtrack to my pain—it was an anthem for my growth.

Part 3: The Soundtrack of Transformation
The transformative and healing power of music.

"Music can heal the wounds that medicine cannot touch."
– Debasish Mridha

The Wall – Pink Floyd

Author: Kian Eder

By the time I was nine years old, I had already experienced a lifetime's worth of pain and turmoil. Abuse, neglect, mental illness, domestic violence, alcoholism, gambling addiction, satanism, pornography, drugs, horror films—you name it, I had witnessed it or been subjected to it. My childhood was anything but ordinary, and the chaos of it all could have easily swallowed me whole. Yet, in the midst of this storm, something within me began to awaken. From about the age of five, I started to observe. I observed the behavior of those around me, the patterns that repeated like a broken record, and the feelings that hung in the air like a heavy fog.

Even at such a young age, I knew deep down that I was here for a reason, that there was something I needed to figure out—some code I needed to crack. I remember thinking to myself, "These people are crazy. Why are they making their lives so hard? Why are they treating each other this way? Why can't they just be happy?" I started to sense the emotions of others, to feel their thoughts as if they were my own. It became clear to me that everyone around me was carrying their own burdens, their own patterns of pain and trauma.

As I observed, I began to understand that the abuse we were

all suffering from was like a disease, passed down from generation to generation. Our parents were unconsciously projecting the pain they had experienced in their own childhoods onto us, just as their parents had done to them, and so on. The cycle seemed endless, and the weight of it all felt suffocating. Despite my mother's constant reassurances that Jesus would come and save us one day, I couldn't shake the feeling *that we needed to save ourselves.*

It was then that I made a decision—one that would shape the course of my life. I told myself, "I have to break this cycle. I don't want to grow up to be a parent who abuses their kids. I have to start working on myself now, so I don't end up like them." At nine years old, I had no idea how I was going to resolve the pain I carried or solve the crisis that was my family life. But I knew, with every fiber of my being, that I had to find a way to release the trauma that was trapped in my body, emotions, and mind. I had to find a way to get it out, to heal.

Then, one night (or should I say morning) everything changed. It was 3 a.m., and I was up watching TV, unable to sleep as usual. The house was silent, save for the low hum of the television and the occasional car passing by. I sat there, a small figure lost in the oversized couch, my eyes glazed over from exhaustion. I was too young to understand the toll that the lack of sleep was taking on my body, but I knew I couldn't rest, not with the nightmares that plagued me every time I closed my eyes.

As I flipped through the channels, desperate for something to distract me from the darkness that loomed in the corners of my mind, a movie came on that seemed dull at first. The intro showed a small boy playing with a rat. He seemed lonely, and I could relate to him immediately. The loneliness in his eyes mirrored my own, and I found myself drawn to the screen. The next scene showed him looking at his father's war medals, feeling estranged and distant, as though the weight of the world was on his tiny shoulders. Again, I related to him, being estranged from my own father. The following scene depicted a mentally ill mother, the emotional distance between them palpable, and an abusive energy that was all too familiar to me.

The movie was *Pink Floyd The Wall,* and for those who have seen it, you'll understand what I mean when I say my nine-year-old mind was blown apart. It was as if someone had taken the thoughts, feelings, and experiences that I had been grappling with and projected them onto the screen. Suddenly, I didn't feel so alone. The music, the lyrics—they spoke directly to me. They were about me. And in that moment, I could feel something inside me begin to heal. The music, oh the music, was so powerful, so epic. It was like nothing I had ever heard before. It resonated deep within me, stirring emotions I didn't even know I had.

The images on the screen were haunting yet mesmerizing. I watched, captivated, as the boy in the movie grew up, his experiences paralleling my own in ways that were both comforting and disturbing. Each scene unfolded like a mirror, reflecting back at me the pain, confusion, and anger that I had buried deep within. I saw myself in that boy, in his struggles, his fears, and his desperate need for escape. But more than that, I saw a way out—a way to transform my pain into something powerful, something *meaningful*.

Through the journey of that movie, I came to a realization that would guide me for the rest of my life: **music could be used as a gateway to healing**. I could turn my darkest feelings into a creation that could help others, that could show people they weren't alone in their struggles. I realized that by becoming a musician, I could channel my pain into something positive, something that could make a difference in the world. I could use music as a tool to help others feel understood, to let them know there was a light amidst the darkness.

As the movie unfolded, the concept of the *"bricks in the wall"* became painfully clear to me. Each traumatic event, each moment of pain and isolation, was like another brick added to the wall that was being built around my heart and soul. The wall was both a defense mechanism and a prison, keeping me safe from the outside world but also trapping me within my own suffering. The abuse, the neglect, the constant turmoil—they were the bricks that separated me from others, that made me feel disconnected and alone. But as I watched, I realized that this wall didn't have to be permanent. It was possible to break it down, to remove the bricks one by one through the power of creativity, through the power of music.

The imagery of the wall resonated deeply with me. It was a physical manifestation of the emotional barriers I had built to protect myself. Every insult, every blow, every moment of abandonment added another layer, another brick, making the wall higher and stronger. And yet, as I watched the protagonist in the movie struggle against his own wall, I understood that these barriers, while protective, were also suffocating. They kept out the pain, but they also kept out the love, the connection, the very things I so desperately needed to heal.

That moment shaped me in so many ways. It gave me a sense of solace, a medicine I could use again and again. Whenever the pain became too much to bear, I would lose myself in music and, in the process, find myself once more. From that day forward, I have been a musician. Not a day goes by that I don't feel that music is an integral part of my healing process. If you listen to my songs, they are dark, but they resolve in the chorus into learning, into wisdom, into awareness. You cannot have the light without the dark; it's essential.

My healing journey has continued ever since that night. Over the years, I have gathered many tools to help me move beyond challenges and become—and continue becoming— the highest version of myself. But creativity, and music in particular, has been the lifeblood of my development. It's the one thing I turned to when I had nothing else. It didn't fix everything, but it helped me process, cope, and survive.

Looking back, I realize that the wall I had built was not just a barrier but a blueprint—a map of the traumas and trials I had endured. Each brick represented a lesson, a truth I had uncovered about myself and the world around me. And while it took years of introspection, inner work, art and music therapy, I began to dismantle that wall, brick by brick. I discovered that behind each layer of pain was a deeper understanding of who I was and what I was capable of.

Creativity became my lifeline, a way to channel the overwhelming emotions that threatened to consume me. When words failed, music spoke. It became my voice, my way of communicating the inexpressible. Through the rhythm and melody, I found a language that could convey the complexities of my inner world in a way that words alone never could. I poured my soul into every note, every chord, transforming my suffering into something beautiful, something that could reach out and touch others who were struggling in their own darkness.

Music was not just a creative outlet; it was a form of rebellion. It was my way of saying, "I will not be defined by my past. I will not be broken by it." In every song I wrote, in every performance, I declared my defiance against the pain, against the despair that sought to drag me down. And in doing so, I found strength—strength I didn't know I had, strength that had been buried beneath the rubble of my broken childhood.

Whatever your creative outlet is, I encourage you to express yourself. Whether it's music, art, cooking, writing, photography, building, inventing, talking, thinking— whatever it looks like for you, do it. Every day, even if it's just for five minutes. It will remind you that you are a creative being, the creator of your life, and that your passions and expressions are essential to what makes you, you.

What's your creative medicine? What is the outlet that allows you to break down the bricks of your own wall? Perhaps you haven't found it yet, or maybe you're still searching for that one thing that resonates with your soul, that gives voice to the silent parts of you that words can't reach. I can't stress enough how vital it is to keep searching, to keep experimenting, until you find that spark—because it's there, waiting to be ignited.

I Saw Her Standing There – The Beatles

Author: Denise VanBriggle

Some of my most vivid memories are of mom, her coal black hair in pin curls, singing along to the radio while she mopped the kitchen floor with Pine Sol and my parents dancing together in just about every room in every house. My dad was dark-haired, too, and a stocky man, but so light on his feet. My mom was tiny, yet her small frame embodied natural rhythm and style. They always looked like they were the happiest people alive when they danced. To my young heart, it seemed as if they had just stepped out of the pages of a fairytale.

In 1963 my parents surprised me, my two teen-aged sisters, and my little sister with the first cabinet-style-mid-century-modern stereo on our block. Our narrow street, lined with duplexes in rows like dominos, was filled with people from diverse backgrounds who truly looked after one another. I can still recall the day the stereo was delivered. It felt like the Second Coming.

Neighbors on both sides of the street stood on their front porches or perched on the railings, almost as excited for its arrival as we were. Their eyes tracked the smooth wooden stereo as it was carried gently out of the truck, down the ramp, up the steps, across the porch, and over the threshold like a new bride.

Inside our home the atmosphere was nothing short of magical anticipation. Daddy had made sure there was an album ready for each one of us. Susie (16) got "Heat Wave" by Martha and the Vandellas; Dianne (13) got "Presenting Dionne Warwick"; My 8-year-old self got "Please Please Me" by the Beatles; and Annette (6) got "Let's All Sing with the Chipmunks." Truth be told, we loved them all. We sat or laid on the floor in front of the speakers for hours on end memorizing the lyrics. We sang and danced to every song on every album, creating a myriad of happy memories.

A particularly potent memory for me includes my best friend, Anne. Not only was she my best friend, but her parents were from England and her whole family knew about The Beatles before anyone in the US. They claimed them as kin, and my young mind assumed they were probably as close as cousins to me as well. I felt like I had the inside scoop on all things British because I spent so much time with Anne and her family. At one point, I think I even started to pick up an accent. Anne's mum always pronounced the word HALF as HOF, so I started saying I wanted just "HOF of this or HOF of that."

When I told Anne's mum about our new stereo and The Beatles album I received, she beamed with pride. "Why don't you bring it the next time you visit, and I'll set up a record player in the basement and you girls can have a DONCE party?" A DONCE party sounded so much more exciting than a "dance" party. The idea excited Anne and me more than you might think. We had been taking DONCE lessons together, so we immediately saw ourselves turning the basement into our own private DONCE studio. We could not have foreseen how pivotal Anne's mum's suggestion would be to our infatuation with all things Beatles.

Our little basement oasis quickly morphed into a bonafide Beatles Fan Club. The two of us and two more neighbor girls transformed ourselves into John, Paul, George, and Ringo after school and on weekends. Anne's mum found inexpensive Beatles wigs for each of us and used huge hat pins to pin them on a large yellow cork board labeled with our names. (She was probably worried about head lice, but we felt like rock stars having our very own wigs in our special recording studio.)

I can still remember the day I took my new "Please Please Me" album to the fan club for the first time. I knew the whole album by heart. I knew Paul sang lead on the opening track of their debut album, so I begged to be Paul on that particular day. The other girls reluctantly agreed because every one of us always wanted to be Paul. He was our collective heartthrob. I often think I learned the importance of fairness in that basement on the days I played the role of John, George, or Ringo. Whoever played George that day put the needle on the record because I had to be ready to belt out an enthusiastic, "One, Two, Three, FAAAA" to get "I Saw Her Standing There" started. If you remember the tune, sing along, won't you?

"Well, she was just seventeen,
You know what I mean,
And the way she looked was way beyond compare,
So how could I dance with another, (WOO)
Oh, when I saw her standing there."

You might recall there was a lot of handclapping and high-pitched "woos" on this track. We mastered them all. And when the "woos" came, we shook our heads and hands vigorously, as any good rockstar would.

Over the years my family's albums grew as our tastes shifted and changed. When a sister left home to start life on her own, she took her records with her. Each of us introduced our cherished music to our boyfriends, spouses, and friends, and our individual collections expanded. Our children and grandchildren inherited a love of music. My mom and dad have been gone for decades, and my sisters and I are all seniors now. When I reflect on our childhood, I thank my parents deeply for this legacy of music. I smile when I think of how the long hours spent around that old stereo forged an unbreakable bond among us that will live on through future generations.

And to this day, whenever I hear "I Saw Her Standing There," I am not on the brink of seventy, writing these words at my kitchen table – I am Paul McCartney standing there in Anne's basement in a Beatles wig, getting ready to belt out *"One, Two, Three, FAAA!"*

Unspoken Word – The Soil

Author: Ruthie Lerato

This song called "Unspoken Word" has no lyrics to guide its theme, yet I feel like I could write a book.

That's the power of music when it hits you in a way that is beyond verbal description. This power of music can bring people together from all walks of life. We find this commonality and eagerly write reflections about how music has affected the very fabric of our lives.

I first heard this song a year or two ago. It was lovely—very impactful and moving. But recently, it brought me to wailing tears in an entirely new experience.

This song revealed my relationship and connection to voices going back generations. Embedded within this rhythm, style, and sound lies the voice of my Sesotho, Zulu, Indian Scottish, yet fully South African, grandmother, Sheila Morifi. She was a vocalist, and a pianist from a family of scholars, much like myself. I could feel my grandmother holding me like a baby through my energetic experience within the song, becoming a portal for grief to pour though.

It brought me to a place beyond just crying and feeling deeply. It catapulted me out of this world and into a gathering of souls I have never met, but I feel connected to in my bones. Even after years of studying and apprenticing with a Brazilian shamanic practitioner, a journey to Peru for Shipibo ceremonial medicine, and a lifetime of being a "deep feeler" ... I have never felt this.

This was me, wailing on my bed, in one of those never ending gut-wrenching cries that I haven't had since I don't know when. The song was on repeat, playing over and over, as I gave myself permission to feel in a direction and depth that I just never felt safe to before—primarily because I didn't want to hurt anyone else's feelings. I rediscovered a story that pulses within me with the prominent urge of a volcano, begging for itself to be heard. I knew in my bones this song was South African. I would bet my life on it.

When I searched online for the origin of the song, I discovered that not only are all of the band members South African—they are from the town of Soweto, the town my family still lives in to this day. It shocked me to discover that there are over 500 small towns in South Africa, and *the artists are from the same exact one as mine.*

However, I have a dual experience. The experience of being American-born, but with parents from other countries... oh honey—it's a thing. My sisters and I understand the comical social blunders we ran into, socializing as 8 year olds calling a headband an *Aliceband*, and taking our first day of school photos decked out in full *Shweshwe cloth* with a matching hat.

Growing up in a home where the World Cup is bigger than the Super Bowl, and pronouncing tomato "toe-MAH-toe," before being socialized in school.

Whenever I don't understand or know of a cultural reference, folks are quick to say *"oh, you're too young."* Actually, I don't know your music reference because my parents are immigrants. This became a joke of sorts that I had with myself. A nurse older than me asks, "Who sings this song?" "Sorry I don't know—my parents are foreign!" I exclaimed, with a laugh in the middle of the Post-Anesthesia Recovery Room. "My parents are foreign" became a running joke consistent in my speech. This all provides comedic relief and social intrigue in my life, transforming an otherwise social blunder into a comfort-zone quip for me.

Despite all of this: what is rarely addressed or understood in American culture, are some of the pains of being a first generation American, or a third-culture-kid. I don't think it's anything ever worth dwelling on or remaining a victim to, as every human has valid grievances of life that can limit our growth. We have to be adaptable in order to survive; this means letting go and focusing on learning, which propels growth. I won't let the hanging truth of *"but we're not victims"* preclude us from accessing meaningful connection and resolution of childhood wounds. Whether you are driven by relationships, health, or career, life has a way of continually bringing you right to the doorstep of your lingering pain that urges to be felt.

If you want to feel free to express your true feelings, or to resonate as deeply and profoundly as the group *The Soil* does with its listeners, drop the armor, listen fully, and reside within the dwelling place of expression. My roommate in 2019 traveled all the way to Europe to see Beethoven. When she finally got to his memorial statue, she was deeply moved to tears. She wept without moving for what felt like hours, purely through his music. I coveted that experience. I never imagined I would have my own version of this, until I had a similar experience in South Africa.

I've been there four times. The earliest memories of my mom and her South African culture are some of the most meaningful moments of my life. Her stark, thick accent caught the attention of Americans, always wondering where she was from. It even compelled my classmates to call my house number and hang up after the voicemail, just to hear my mom's "cool accent." I'll always have the memory of the smelling curry masala, chopped ginger, and garlic drifting from our kitchen. My mom has been invited to various schools, churches, and presentations as a storyteller, particularly for children, bringing her drums, masks, beads, and books. These are some of my favorite memories of my mom.

In college, I was nominated and became the president of my college's Black Student Union. I carry a mix of shame and pride with that decision. Why pride? I truly felt I was the perfect person to do the job, because I understood many perspectives, growing up in a black neighborhood, with foreign parents, but attending a predominantly white school with almost all white friends. I was always the oddball, never fit in, but could sympathize with all perspectives. I said yes because I was confident in the depth of heart I possess for everyone - both white and black students, and everyone in between; to hopefully see the naked truth within themselves and each other: That we're all the same, and we're all different. Let's honor both.

But then there was shame. Why shame? There are benefits to having a group like a Black Student Union, which is something that has existed for decades in many colleges all throughout the country. For me, the open-dialogue processing and understanding of racial identity, and the deconstruction of internalized racism, radically changed my life. It has brought me peace, compassion, and understanding. And it has released me from the inferiority complex and self-victimization I carried as a child in a predominantly white school. I just needed a safe, dedicated space to openly talk about it.

However, I am also aware that this is only one step in the direction of harmonic peace. I recognize that by the name alone, Black Student Union unintentionally excludes the very people who need to be welcomed into the conversation. Furthermore, it perpetuates the idea of a scary Black Panther-like movement that evokes fear in others who haven't yet heard the truth of what goes on there. Similar to how men could perhaps perceive a "Women's Circle" gathering as exclusive and a place for men-bashing, when in reality, that couldn't be further from the truth. It is a place to gather and share relatable experiences, support each other, and lift each other up for the purpose of personal growth, self-awareness, and empowerment. It is love and community in action.

We need open hearted talks, without the need to defend or protect anyone's victim story, while at the same time still addressing and validating why one could easily feel left out, intimidated, or fearful. We can clear up the divisions and illusions propagated on TV our whole lives and connect in a way that is more compassionate and evolved, rather than fighting, ridiculing, and killing one another.

The details matter to me because something as seemingly insignificant as hair texture has shaped the fate of my family. I've undoubtedly benefited from white privilege more than most, because I wouldn't have been born if my mother hadn't "ranked high" in the political caste system Apartheid. In apartheid South Africa, race wasn't an optional box to check off—it was mandatory, documented in a personal passbook (like an ID card) that dictated your rights, much like a caste system. Your race determined your access to schools, parks, housing, and more, enforced by a rigid hierarchy: Those classified as White carried the most access to society, such as universities, hospitals and parks, followed then by Coloreds, Indians, and then Blacks/Africans.

My mom fell under the category of Colored at age 4 when apartheid was ramping up, judging by the way her hair curled and because her skin is quite fair. Could you imagine being four years old and sitting with police, holding a projector up against your facial profile, to judge which access to citizenship you will receive? The woman who carries the grief of these memories is the woman who carried me. And thus, when hearing "Unspoken Word," the grief came back like a memory through my very cells, and I knew this song was a lament of Soweto. *The Soil* claims to simply be channels of the songs that they believe come to them from a sacred place, serving as mediums that help carry the message. Two generations later, I heard the message, loud and clear.

To receive a proper education, my mother wore a headwrap on the bus during her long commute to school, allowing her to pass as Colored and avoid the inferior Bantu education imposed on Black Africans and Indians. This system was deliberately designed to limit opportunities for non-White South Africans. Eventually, she managed to leave South Africa. Her darker-skinned African brother, however, was not as fortunate. He never escaped, and he is no longer alive today. Yet, here I am—I exist because of the perception of my mother's skin color and hair texture at that time. If my mother hadn't escaped in the 1980s, aided by the higher education she received as someone "white-passing enough" to access better opportunities, she might never have become an international traveling nurse. And without that, I would not exist.

I don't share this out of pride but out of anger. Personally, I have technically benefited from racism directly, yet I've also been deeply hurt by it at the same time. What a conundrum to live with, indeed. I often wonder what it would've been like to grow up with my South African family. Everyone but my mom is back in South Africa, and I am mysteriously missing from the family, out here living my best life going to private schools. Oh, the guilt. The cost of this glorious life I now live is preceded by family members that were tortured and killed—some whose names I'll never know. My mother grew up caring for her mentally ill mother, a burden she bore as a child. Our farmland was stolen, and with it, much of our personal history, leaving us with few photos or possessions to connect to our heritage. Long before her physical death, apartheid in the 1960s broke her spirit. She had a nervous breakdown, losing her ability to sing, perform, and host the gatherings my mother cherished. For decades, she battled mental illness, cared for lovingly by my grandfather until she passed.

Why did she lose herself? Living under an unjust system that devalues your very existence torments the soul. Ignoring these lived experiences only deepens wounds and division. The grief is layered: families denied quality education, housing, and even basic utilities like electricity, all while the government ensured others had access. Such petty injustices symbolize a far greater cruelty.

But to me, the much greater grief lies within the crushed soul that prevented my grandmother from singing ever again. It prevented her from being able to make music again. It denied her the ability to even throw parties as she used to as a frequent host of local events. To squander out the music, is to squander out the soul. It can thwart even the most vibrant spirit from accessing the passion, the heart, and the will to live in beautiful harmony. But thoughts regarding any of this to this day remain unspoken, too exhausting and deep to address in a casual conversation. And let's be honest— talking about these topics aloud would make people uncomfortable. And I think that's why the artists created such a title for such a powerful song.

This is precisely what's given me so much faith and courage to be myself, even in the face of self-doubt or fear. I express myself openly, publicly, and vulnerably as a privilege that my family did not get access to. Each time I share a podcast, share my music and voice, or my thoughts in an online post— I do so with the feeling of breakthrough and celebration that apartheid is now, officially, over. A dream that kept Mandela in prison for 27 years. A generation of struggle that made way for someone you and I to remember humanity, and make a difference.

I hope to remind us that we have permission to feel fully, while also striking the chord of balance, to simultaneously listen and hear others fully as well. To express our hearts' song, while also taking accountability to choose courageous love every time, even in the face of fear.

I took on roles in student leadership for this purpose: to help us remember that our words and actions affect one another. It doesn't matter if you're black or white. We are all one. We all have had our grievances, and these are valid, for every human that has ever existed. If it's eating you up inside, do not let them remain Unspoken.

Address and settle these grievances through speaking and expressing yourself, boldly and shamelessly. Pair this with listening to each other, deeply and fully. Your truth rests within your bones, before you even lift your voice to speak.

We find the answers to what we've been looking for when we're finally ready to listen. And to feel, fully - without resistance. That is what I experienced when I felt and listened to this song. When I listened all the way, with every fiber of my being, until the dots all connected – I felt the unspoken lament of my grandmother—a cry she never got to release. For her, it remains Unspoken. But for me, to freely express myself is the most priceless gift I could've been given.

It is through the shadow that we find our greatest gifts.
It's through the soil, the dirt, the darkness that we find the light. It takes willingness to hear, be heard, and forgive endlessly.

And I have found no true peace any other way.

The Sign - Nujabes ft. Pase Rock

Author: Brett Ward

As I approach my 30s, I find myself in a space where experiences and philosophies are beginning to converge. My worldview feels less blurry, and I've started to find clarity about how I see the world and how I hope it could be. It's a process I think many of us go through—a gradual shaping of our perspectives through exploration and growth. For me, music, especially hip hop, has always been a tool to process this inner space.

Hip hop, in its many iterations, reflects the connection between ourselves and the world around us. It's a lens, a translation, and sometimes a way to make sense of things that feel chaotic or overwhelming. When I feel disconnected, misunderstood, or even burdened by what I see in the world, I turn to hip hop as a way to understand and reconnect. The way it dissects ideas, arranges words, and gives voice to struggles is a cathartic process. It reminds me that I'm not the only one who sees the cracks in the facade of society.

There's something about the way hip hop blends rhythm and thought, music and emotion, that feels like it's tapping into a deeper truth. It allows for complexity—it doesn't shy away from the hard questions. For me, it's not just music; it's a companion in my efforts to make sense of the world, to

156

process the things that don't sit right, and to build something meaningful from the pieces.

"The Sign" by Nujabes has been one of the most important songs in helping me navigate this space. Its repetitive questioning and poetic style have a meditative quality, creating moments of reflection every time I hear it. It isn't a hopeful song—it's actually quite pessimistic—but it has taught me to find purpose even within that pessimism. It's a reminder to acknowledge the grief in the world without turning away from it, to hold space for awareness even when it feels heavy.

The song brings to mind the idea of omens—the signs of a world that's in trouble. Pase Rock speaks about things we often avoid thinking about: environmental destruction, societal collapse, and a culture consumed by materialism. He shares his frustration with seeing these signs when others don't seem to notice or care. That frustration resonates deeply with me. In a world where we can learn of a new tragedy every minute, it's easy to feel overwhelmed or powerless.

But sometimes, it's in those moments of overwhelming awareness that we start to see clearly. "The Sign" doesn't offer solutions, but it pushes me to ask the hard questions: What kind of world are we creating? What do we want to leave behind for the next generation? What can I do, even if it feels small?

It's easy to feel like our individual actions don't matter, especially when we're up against systems and structures that seem immovable. But the way I see it, awareness itself is a form of resistance. Just recognizing the cracks in the system, refusing to look away, is a way of saying, "I see this, and it's not okay." That's where change starts—not with answers, but with the willingness to see the problem and sit with it.

We live in a world of endless distractions. Some distractions are necessary—working to provide for ourselves and our families, for example—but others keep us from facing the larger issues that demand our attention. Listening to this song reminds me to pause and reflect on what's truly in front of me and how I can protect it for the future. It's not about solving every problem or carrying the weight of the world alone. Sometimes it's as simple as staying aware, as being present and alive to the reality we live in.

The systems we've created often feel like they're working against us, driving environmental destruction, inequality, and exploitation. Yet, even in the face of these massive challenges, there's something powerful about trying—about doing what we can, however small it may feel.

There's no denying the challenges we face. As a society, we've prioritized profit over people and convenience over sustainability. We've built systems that encourage short-term gains at the expense of long-term consequences. And the worst part is, most of us don't even want this. Who among us is asking for polluted rivers, for ecosystems on the brink of collapse, for communities devastated by exploitation? Yet these are the realities we face because of choices made by systems that prioritize wealth over well-being.

"The Sign" doesn't offer solutions. It doesn't pretend everything will be okay. But it pushes me to think about what I can do in my own space and time. It's a reminder that every action, no matter how small, has value. Whether it's being mindful of waste, supporting local communities, or simply staying present, these choices matter.

There's no guarantee that we can undo the damage, but we owe it to ourselves—and to future generations—to try. I find comfort in knowing I'm not alone in seeing these signs and wanting to act on them. Each time I hear the song, I feel a little less isolated, a little more connected to others who are also navigating this complicated, imperfect world.

The truth is, we're all just trying to make sense of the signs around us. Maybe that's all we can do—stay awake, stay aware, and do our best to create a future we'd want to be a part of.

Rocky Mountain High - John Denver

Author: Jeanne Edwards

It was the summer of 1984. My family spent a month traveling cross country from our home in New Jersey to the West Coast in California. We traveled in our Oldsmobile Cutlass station wagon which was packed to the gills with the personal effects for my parents, brother, sister, and me. We were also outfitted with a Sears X-Cargo clamshell cargo holder and a soft pack on the roof rack which held the gear that we would use to camp at various sites along our journey.

One item that I am so grateful that we had the foresight to pack was our battery-operated General Electric cassette player that played the music which became the soundtrack for our road trip and all the memories we made. I distinctly remember one particular cassette tape that was played repeatedly as we explored the beauty of the National Parks...John Denver's Greatest Hits. It included a compilation of songs that have become anthems to rouse and uplift me during key moments both on this trip as well as in life.

One of my first core memories was listening to the song "Rocky Mountain High" while witnessing the snowcapped peaks of the Rockies soaring high into the clouds amid summer, while I was simultaneously dwarfed by the towering Douglas Firs and Ponderosa Pines. While in Rocky

Mountain National Park, we 'climbed Cathedral Mountains and journeyed along Trail Ridge Road until we arrived where 'you saw everything as far as you can see.' Before exiting the car, I donned my hiking boots and a sweatshirt because, while it was mid-summer, we were in the alpine tundra, the land above the trees.

As I opened the car door, I was enveloped by crisp cool mountain air. It invigorated me as we set out on our hike. The terrain was different from anything I had experienced. There were ground-hugging clumps of moss, lichens clinging to rocks and Alpine Paintbrush, Phlox and Forget-Me-Not, which all added pops of color amongst the gray, green and brown terrain. This was my first foray into an elevation over 11,000 feet; yet, I felt comforted and welcomed as if 'coming home to a place (I've) never been before.'

My encounters with this monumental landscape were both thrilling and deeply moving, just as Denver's music was to my soul. These combined experiences allowed my eight-year-old self to be filled with a sense of wonder.

I remember another particular stop at Bear Lake in Estes, Colorado. The sheer size and grandeur of the mountains made a lasting impression on me and transformed my, then, child's view of the world and my place within it. My dad snapped two photos of me as I stared at the 'serenity of a clear blue mountain lake' with Hallett Peak, or what is known as Bonoh'ooonoteyoon by the Arapaho, in the background.

The song "Rocky Mountain High," is imbued with a sense of reverence and awe for the natural beauty of the mountains and portrays them as a place of spiritual elevation and personal renewal. The lyrics to the song illuminate Denver's own personal Rocky Mountain experience. It occurred late in the evening on a mid-summer moonless night as he was camped out near an alpine lake under a starlit sky during the Perseid meteor shower. The lyric, 'rainin' fire in the sky' was his offering to memorialize his experience. My personal appreciation for summer campouts – contemplating near bodies of water under the Perseids, as well as moments in nature where one can walk 'in quiet solitude (through) the forests and the streams' – has only continued to expand following my introduction to both these landscapes as well as Denver's music.

By framing the mountains as a place of emotional and spiritual elevation, Denver's song aligns with a broader cultural narrative that seeks to find meaning and renewal through engagement with the natural world. Mountains have long represented various aspects of the human experience including challenges, aspirations, transformation, strength, power, freedom and resilience in overcoming obstacles and challenges.

In June 2018, I found myself heading back to the West Coast, but this time I was traveling to Bakersfield, California. I was meeting up with my mother, father and sister as we, individually and collectively, tried to find the strength to retrieve my brother's cremated remains following his unexpected passing two weeks earlier. My brother self-identified as a Geologist, Giga Pan photographer, educator, alpha geek and explorer. He was passionate about nature and geoscience, likely enhanced by our cross-country trip in the summer of 1994, and he shared this passion with everyone he interacted with.

While my previous journey out West, as a child, had me filled with excitement and a true fervor for life, this trip, as an adult, found me numb and challenged to find a new way to show up in the world following the death of my brother. During this trip, I had a layover in Denver and as my plane left the airport, I was awakened out of my mournful slumber. As I looked out the window, I witnessed a beautiful sunset over the Rocky Mountains. able to bear witness to a serene sunset as we flew over the Rocky Mountains. Then, as if my brother had shuffled the playlist himself, "Rocky Mountain High" streamed through my headphones and right into my soul.

In many traditions, mountains are identified as sacred places, believed to be closer to the Divine. Their towering presence and serene expanses often induce a profound feeling of awe and wonder, which can be interpreted as a glimpse into something greater than the everyday human experience. Mountains, by their sheer scale and the majestic solitude they offer, invite contemplation and introspection. This was certainly my experience. These types of encounters with the sublime often prompt a deeper reflection on existence as well as one's place within it. In the presence of a mountain, we are encouraged to ponder the vastness of the universe and our own capacity for inner growth and exploration.

The formidable heights of mountains can represent the aspiration to reach beyond ordinary limits, suggesting a journey towards a higher state of being or understanding. Climbing or even gazing upon these peaks can evoke a sense of striving towards something profound and ineffable, reinforcing the idea that there are dimensions of experience and knowledge that transcend our usual perceptions.

Many have long believed that the 'Rocky Mountain High' was all about getting stoned in the mountains. While John Denver acknowledged that such activities were indeed going on, he shared that the song was about living and experiencing what humans were created for – freedom – and "how exhilarating it was to be there, to feel free, to have come to such a place, both personally and geographically. And it was a reflection on mortality."

The isolation of mountains can create a natural sanctuary, a place removed from the usual chaos of daily life. People go to the mountains to get away from it all...or is it actually to be better able to tune into it all? This separation from the everyday world allows individuals the opportunity to experience a heightened state of consciousness or awareness. As one becomes more aware, they see the irony of how the vastness and enduring nature of mountains symbolize both stability and permanence; something that is contrasted sharply with the ephemeral nature of human existence. Yet, we are all connected.

From the rhythmic cycles of the seasons influencing our moods to the calming presence of forests, rivers, and mountains that provide solace and inspiration; the natural world acts as both backdrop and catalyst for our experience as well as the songs and stories we share. We find connection and meaning in the changing landscapes, which provide us moments to reflect on our own journeys of growth, resilience, and transformation. Whether it's the thrill of a sunrise or the serenity of a starlit sky; nature's beauty invites us to pause, reflect, and appreciate our place within a larger ecosystem, reminding us that we are part of something far greater than ourselves.

Music and nature share a profound connection, with each influencing and inspiring the other in countless ways. The sounds of the natural world—birds singing, leaves rustling in the wind, or the gentle rush of a stream—often serve as the foundation for musical expression, echoing the rhythms and melodies found in the wild. Many musicians and songwriters draw from nature's beauty, translating its nuances into harmonies and lyrics that resonate deeply with the human spirit. The interplay between music and nature enriches our lives, inviting us to experience the world with heightened awareness and appreciation.

This particular anthem has both encouraged me to be in nature and supported me in times of difficulty as I learn to be myself. All aspects of these combined experiences – the music, nature and learning who I am as part of this world – have truly been a balm for my soul. Even when I can't get out into nature or tune into music, I am fortunate to be able to tune into the visual of my contemplative moment staring up at Hallett Peak, which continues to be the happy place that I go to in my mind's eye and reminds me of my connection to the interconnection of it all.

Happy – Pharrel Williams

Author: Michelle Wolfe

There are few songs that have the ability to transform a mood instantaneously, and for me, "Happy" by Pharrell Williams is one of them. Every time I hear the upbeat melody and the infectious claps, something in my body just shifts. It doesn't matter if I'm feeling stressed, overwhelmed, or just neutral— when Pharrell sings, *"clap along if you feel like happiness is the truth,"* I am moved, I can't help but clap along, and I feel it.

This song has become a kind of personal anthem, a musical trigger that reminds me of joy, movement, and the power of music to change my internal state. My kids laugh at me when they see me belting out the lyrics, clapping, or moving my body in sync with the beat, especially while I'm driving, but I don't care. It makes me happy. And more importantly, it reminds me that happiness is something I can choose, something I can cultivate, and that music is a tool to access it instantly.

Music and the Mind-Body Connection

The impact of "Happy" on my mood isn't just anecdotal—it's deeply rooted in science. Music has a profound effect on the brain, the nervous system, and overall well-being. Neuroscientists have found that when we listen to music, especially uplifting and rhythmic songs, our brains release dopamine, a neurotransmitter associated with pleasure and reward. This explains why hearing the first few notes of a song we love can immediately trigger a sense of excitement or nostalgia.

Beyond dopamine, music also influences cortisol levels, which are associated with stress. Listening to upbeat music has been shown to reduce cortisol, leading to lower stress levels and an overall sense of relaxation. This is why music is often used in therapy, meditation, and even hospital settings to help patients manage pain and anxiety.

In the case of "Happy," the song's tempo, clapping rhythm, and major key all work together to create a sense of upliftment. The beat sits at around 160 beats per minute (BPM), which aligns with an energetic and motivational pace—something that naturally encourages movement. Whether you're tapping your foot, nodding your head, or dancing in your car, the body wants to respond. And when the body moves, it further reinforces the *feel-good effect* through the release of endorphins.

The Psychological Power of Music

Music's ability to shift emotions is well-documented in psychology. In cognitive behavioral therapy (CBT), for example, there is an emphasis on reframing thoughts to change emotional responses. Music naturally does this without effort. A sad song can make us cry, while an upbeat song like "Happy" can make us feel joy in an instant. This is because music has direct access to the limbic system — the part of the brain responsible for processing emotions. Unlike spoken words, which require cognitive effort to interpret, music bypasses the rational mind and goes straight to the emotional core.

Studies have shown that people who listen to music intentionally to regulate their emotions experience greater psychological resilience. They are able to use music as a tool for self-soothing, motivation, and even catharsis. For me, "Happy" is my reset button. When I'm feeling sluggish, irritable, or distracted, I put it on, and within seconds, my state shifts.

One of the reasons "Happy" is so effective at shifting mood is because it encourages movement. The link between music and movement is so strong that even individuals who struggle with motor function, such as Parkinson's patients, have been shown to move more fluidly when listening to rhythmic music. This is because music activates motor areas of the brain, synchronizing movement with sound in a way that feels almost automatic.

When we move in response to music, we engage in what neuroscientists call *entrainment*. This phenomenon refers to the brain's natural tendency to synchronize with external rhythms. Entrainment not only improves coordination and motor function but also plays a role in emotional regulation. It's why dancing, exercising, or even just clapping along to a song can feel so liberating. Movement releases stored tension in the body, making it a natural way to process stress and emotions.

I've noticed this in my own experience. When I hear "Happy" while driving, I find myself tapping on the steering wheel, bobbing my head, or even full-on dancing at a red light (much to the amusement of my kids and other drivers). The simple act of moving, even in small ways, reinforces the joy that the song brings. It's a reminder that I can shift my emotional state at any time through movement and music.

The Social and Cultural Impact of "Happy"

Beyond personal experience, "Happy" has had a global impact. Released in 2013 as part of the Despicable Me 2 soundtrack, the song quickly became an anthem of joy, topping charts worldwide and even inspiring the United Nations to declare March 20th as the International Day of Happiness. The song's universal appeal lies in its simplicity—it's easy to sing along to, easy to move to, and easy to feel uplifted by.

The music video itself became a movement, with people from all walks of life submitting their own versions of the song, dancing and expressing their joy. This speaks to something fundamental about music—it has the power to connect people across cultures, backgrounds, and experiences. The communal aspect of music is deeply ingrained in human history, from tribal drumming to modern-day concerts. Music is a shared experience, and songs like "Happy" serve as collective reminders of joy and unity.

Recognizing music's ability to shift emotions and regulate the nervous system, I've started using it more intentionally in my daily life. Whether it's curating playlists for different moods, using music to start my morning with energy, or playing calming sounds before bed, I see music as a tool for self-care.

For anyone looking to harness music's power, here are some practical ways to use it for emotional well-being:

- Create Mood-Based Playlists: Have a "Happy" playlist for when you need a boost, a "Calm" playlist for winding down, and a "Motivation" playlist for workouts or productivity.

- Move with Music: Whether it's dancing, walking, or even stretching, pairing movement with music amplifies its benefits.

- Use Music for Mindfulness: Listening to music with full presence—paying attention to the instruments, lyrics, and emotions it evokes—can be a form of meditation.

- Sing Out Loud: Singing, even if you're off-key, releases stress and stimulates the vagus nerve, which promotes relaxation.

- Let Music Be a Companion: Just as "Happy" is my go-to song for lifting my spirits, find songs that act as anchors for different emotional states.

Music, at its core, is energy in motion. It affects our brains, our bodies, and our emotions in ways that science is still uncovering. "Happy" by Pharrell Williams is just one example of how a song can become a personal tool for transformation. For me, it's a reminder that happiness is a choice, that movement is medicine, and that joy is always within reach—sometimes all it takes is a beat, a clap, and a song.

So, if you ever find yourself needing a lift, try it. Play "Happy." Clap along. Move your body. And see how quickly music can turn your mood around.

Because happiness is, indeed, the truth.

Beautiful Dawn - The Wailin Jennys
Author: Murshida VA

Wonderful-Terrible. ~Sufi Saying

Moving meditation,
ecstatic contemplation
Breathing revelation,
Sound,
Devotion,
Invocation.

The angels come,
They sing with us,[1] *it's said…*

Again and again, again and again…
Until everything and nothing are one
Until everything and nothing are one

---

[1] Ancient Dervish (Sufi) ritual. *"Zikr may be called the finest thought expressed in the finest material form with the highest spiritual purpose. It becomes the perfection of the sounds uttered by the tongue.* -Hazrat Inayat Khan. Zikr, meaning remembrance, is the most essential practice in Sufism. This sentiment is as true for the Inayatiyya as for all other Sufi paths. From the mystical point of view, all of life, the universe, and existence is One. The source, goal, and substance of all beings is The One, The Eternal, The Infinite, Divine Being. And yet, we may forget this essential reality, believing throughout our lives that we are only this limited set of sensations, memories, thoughts, roles, and self-identities. Fortunately, the soul's desire to remember its true being cannot be ignored. Throughout the millennia, mystics in all traditions have developed practices aimed at recovering and remembering that vast, boundless aspect of our being. For the Sufis, that central practice is called *zikr*, its primary formulation, *La ilaha illa'llah (Nothing exists but The One)*. See: Zikr

Again and again, again and again…
Until nothing is left of us except…

The One

Sound and heat, skin and breath,
Again, again, again…

A song on repeat
Until the angels come…

I loved him beyond reason or hope. I loved him all at once, without knowing who or why, as if my love had always been. A light in a cave revealing eternity. That. A force without beginning or end. That. As absurdly and irresistibly irrational as that. Choiceless. Chosen. Beyond choosing. That. And so naive, I had no idea it was personal. Sexual. Or would be. Could be. I was simply sleepless, sobbing, praying through tears and snot—for him to be well, to be healed, to be happy, to be free—for his heart to know joy again.

For his heart to know peace…

I had no idea he was outside my door. No idea an angel had come to bring him home from hell. No idea an angel had pierced his heart and returned him to himself. No idea an angel had come, just as the ancients said angels will come, as Murshid said angels will come.

On the Zikr…

I didn't know until he told me, himself, three days later. He looked like a different man. His eyes, once sunken and dark, sparkling with life.

A year later, we were together.

Ahhh, but my patterns of attraction to men have always been…

Difficult.

And so it was, in the end, he turned away, leaving me to face the very real possibility of life in prison—without him. Without his comfort, without his presence.

A hard teacher, that man.

What does not kill us makes us stronger.

That.

And so it was that, in late October of 2013, I found myself, alone, driving 1,682 miles from his desert shack in Truth or Consequences, NM, to the Evans Courthouse in Richmond County, GA. For three days, I drove, sleeping in parking lots, eating what little I could afford, and, to soothe my heart, playing "Beautiful Dawn" by the Wailin' Jennys. "Beautiful Dawn" on repeat...

Beautiful Dawn.
The whole time.
Even in my sleep.

And singing, and singing, and singing, until—

Tears and snot rolled down my cheeks.

Again.
And again.
And again.

Beautiful Dawn.
on repeat...

Maybe my heart opened so wide, so wide, as I sang and wept my way to Georgia, that the angels took pity on me...

Maybe my broken-open surrender, in the midst of pain and fear and courage, moved the angel so deeply that an Inner Way opened a Mystery...

That *Beautiful Dawn* became a Zikr...

Maybe the angels sent him to me.

For, suddenly, there I was, both driving and whirling[2]...

Whirling, whirling, whirling...

With the judge.

I had never met the judge, so I assumed I was imagining his blue eyes twinkling at me through wire glasses, hands holding mine, robes flying out behind him...

Whirling, whirling, whirling...

To "Beautiful Dawn."

I had defied the law. Consciously. Without violence, and with intent to change it. Civil Disobedience.

That.

---

[2] The Indigenous Peoples call this Doubling. It is the ability to be in two planes, or even two places, at once, The Indigenous consider this a Shamanic gift. The Yogis call this a Siddhi. And all paths who still recall the existence of what we commonly call extraordinary human capacities, also agree: these gifts may come in response to a need arising from within that person when the needs of the individual and the needs of the collective are one. As such they are gifts, blessings showered upon us, to be neither commanded nor controlled. They are grace. And yes, there are yogis who are blessed with the ability to command a specific Siddhi or Siddhis but that ability is few and far between and also given as a gift. As Grace.

But in those days, nobody talked about Civil Disobedience anymore. Or "innocent until proven guilty."

"We start in a hole," my lawyer told me during our first hearing together. "We have to dig ourselves out."

"What happened to 'innocent until proven guilty'?" I asked.

He sighed and looked at me in silence. Then he looked away.

He was young, handsome, upright—yet already resigned, already cynical. His words fell like stones into my stomach. The burden wasn't on the prosecution. It was on us. It was on us in this place that reeked of corruption. I wondered what influence an honest law firm could wield in such a cesspool of trickery and deceit. I was about to learn: almost none.

To be clear, I was guilty. That wasn't the issue. I came to change the law, and at that moment, I stood in the hood in Augusta, GA, with 26 pounds of AAA Cali Medical in the trunk.

When the officer asked, "What's your profession, ma'am?"

I told the truth: "I'm a spiritual guide."

I am so fucked.

Not necessarily, said the Guidance.

There was no one physically there, but I knew that voice. I trusted it.

This trial—had it been about justice—would not have been about whether I was guilty or not guilty. It would have been about whether convicting anyone of nonviolent cannabis offenses served justice. It would have been a trial turning on the power of Jury Nullification, the absurdities of the War on Drugs, and the encroaching totalitarianism of Mass Incarceration.

I was sent to change the law.

Don't say that out loud. Not yet.

People think spiritual leadership is fun. They forget Jean d'Arc, MLK, Gandhi. Jesus, for fuck's sake. Jesus. What I was doing was much smaller than that. My battlefield was a courtroom, my speech a few words at a podium. And my life was at stake in a way that very few people could even understand. People often fail to connect the dots, but connecting dots has always been my gift, so I was terrified. Defiant and terrified and determined. And terrified.

A friend once told me, "I've seen you go all the way to the edge of insanity, yet, somehow, you never quite cross the line."

Just a hair shy of bat shit crazy. Just a hair shy of a wall covered in photographs and strings delineating nonsense. I will never know why I was blessed with the ability to venture so far out into wildly trippy places (with and without drugs), and yet, somehow, remain anchored, one toe planted firmly this side of irretrievably lost to meaningless chaos.

The line between personal spiritual ecstasy and insanity is membranously thin. ~Pir Vilayat

That.

And then, as if all of this wasn't already enough to deal with, God, who, as the saying goes, obviously thought I was a badass, decided to up the ante by tossing irresistible mystical passion and supernatural romance into the mix. Holy hell. Great. Terrific. Thanks a lot, Dude. Just what I needed. Facepalm.

So, there I was, raw and open-hearted and proverbial balls to the proverbial wall, face down on the February gravel in Augusta, GA, bleeding and cold—with a cop on my back.

Shit.

Of course, I didn't realize he was a cop, at first, and that, that, too, is a story for another time…

Twenty months after my arrest—on the morning of October 23, 2013—I sat behind the wheel of my dead mother's midnight-blue Scion, selected "Beautiful Dawn" on the stereo, and pressed repeat.

Take me to a place where courage doesn't have a name...

For three days, I drove.
"Beautiful Dawn."
The whole time.
Even in my sleep.

Singing, and singing, and singing, until—
Tears and snot rolled down my cheeks.
Again.
And again.
And again.

Maybe my heart opened so wide that the angels mistook "Beautiful Dawn" for a Zikr. Maybe the angels took pity on my trembling and chose to walk with me into that courthouse.

Or maybe this really was a calling from God.

Lord knows there were signs. From the very beginning there were signs. Inexplicable synchronicity after inexplicable synchronicity. The way magic and destiny work. That.

And "Beautiful Dawn" was my defiant joy. "Beautiful Dawn" was my "Hallelujah anyway"[3].

The night before sentencing, I danced. On the streets of Augusta, I danced. With tears streaming down my face, I danced. I danced in defiance. I danced in joy. I danced forgiveness and love for all the broken hearted people who were left with nothing inside them but judgement and hate, for all the broken hearted people who had given up the dreams of their innocence and resigned to the inevitability of living one lie after another until they lost the ability to tell truth from fiction, until they actually believed they were doing something right and good. And I danced to bring the courage up inside of my own body until it filled my heart and bolstered my spirit with the strength to walk into that courtroom in the morning.

And then I quietly walked into the bed and breakfast that welcomed me each time I traveled to Augusta, opened the door to room 5, took a long hot shower and crawled into bed, listening to the echoes of "Beautiful Dawn" on repeat. The echoes, no longer in the room, but in my soul.

I arrived at the Courthouse in Evans, GA early, a small miracle for me, and the judge was nearly two hours late. When he finally entered the courtroom, he walked past me, paused, almost imperceptibly, nodded hello. I looked up into

---

[3] See: https://www.michellenezat.com/podcast-469-hallelujah-anyway-by-rend-collective

the face of the man in my vision, the man who had been holding my hands for hours as I drove, the man who was whirling with me, to Beautiful Dawn.

Two more hours later, almost the last to be called, I stood at the podium in the criminal courthouse in Evans, GA, silent. Until the judge invited me to speak my name. I leaned toward the mic and the sound of my voice hit the sweet spot, sending my name echoing through the courtroom...

Angela, Angela, Angela....

Echoing...

Reverberating...

Inexplicable...

Perhaps I was suddenly in a different form of time than almost all of the people in the room. Beside me, to the left of the podium, I felt my attorney's body jerk, again, almost imperceptibly. I turned and glanced up and around me to see the Court Recorder and the DA jerk in exactly the same way. Everything seemed to be in slow motion, except for me... And the judge...

It looked like waves of sound were penetrating everyone in the courtroom and triggering some kind of cosmic reset button. An image of a red or white circuit breaker button on the back of a 1960's television set floated into my awareness. I look up at the judge. He was looking straight at me, smiling...

For a moment, he and I were the only two people in the room, and then just as suddenly and inexplicably as the phenomenon had arisen, it vanished, and everything seemed business as usual again.

There's science now — hard science — confirming the power of words and music to shape the brain's pathways. Studies show how uplifting music can release dopamine, elevate consciousness, and ripple through our communities.

For me, it's simpler than that.

When a stone skips across the surface of a lake,

The ripples —
Touch everything.

That.

In the courtroom that day my voice became that stone.

What came after...

What the ripples touched and changed and how those changes unfolded...

That, too, is a story for another day. What matters in this moment is:

I didn't choose to make those ripples with my voice. I didn't intend to hit the sweet spot on that mic. I didn't imagine making a sound that pierced and healed the stone cold hearts of men. I didn't invoke that Siddhi to accomplish a wonder in that courtroom. It just happened. The judge invited me, and the sound just happened. The angels came, the mystery opened, and the sound moved through space as ripples moved across and through a lake...

Changing everything...

And as I write this, I wonder:

What are those ripples changing now? What sound is rippling through the realms of Creation? What breath? How does birdsong dance with the wind through leaves and forests, with the wind whirling around the mountains? How does sound sustain and change our world? How does one child's laughter rise to the heavens, bringing joy to the Angels, the Ancestors, and the Clouds? How does the Sky feel when we cry out in joy or wail and keen, inconsolable, grieving, tears and snot running down our faces, breath jagged in our chests? What echoes will our brief lives make within the vastness of Creation?

And "Beautiful Dawn…"

"Beautiful Dawn" was my Zikr. "Beautiful Dawn" was my courage and my defiant joy. "Beautiful Dawn" was my *Hallelujah, Anyway*.

To "Beautiful Dawn."
To the liberation of all beings.
Toward the One.

Maybe It's Just Me – Butch Walker

Author: Scott Lester

Love... is a tricky bitch. Sometimes we know we're in it, but what we don't know is what to do about it. One of the truest forms of love is putting someone else's happiness above your own, and that's exactly what "Maybe It's Just Me" explores. It's not an idea that gets much airtime in our culture, where love songs are often all about *me, me, me*. But Butch Walker's take on love flips the script, offering a selfless perspective that's rare and gut-wrenching.

This year marks the twentieth anniversary of *"Letters,"* the album that houses this gem of a song. It's a brilliant collection of bittersweet anthems—snapshots of heartbreak, longing, and the complicated reality of relationships. While not the record that introduced me to Walker's music, it's the one that made me a devoted fan. As a musician and songwriter, myself, *"Letters"* became a masterclass in storytelling, melody, and emotional resonance. It's the kind of album that reminds you how powerful music can be when it taps into something raw and universal.

"Maybe It's Just Me" stands out because it starts where most love songs end—with the breakup. The relationship is over. One partner has moved on, and the other is left trying to make sense of the aftermath. The narrator reflects on the painful reality of seeing the person they love genuinely happy—happier, it seems, without them. It's a brutally honest look at closure, the kind we don't want but sometimes have to face.

The song captures the aching tension of wanting someone to be happy while grappling with the fact that their happiness no longer includes you. It's the kind of bittersweet realization that feels like a punch to the gut. As the narrator observes the joy on their former partner's face, there's a mix of pride and heartbreak. You want to celebrate their newfound glow, their freedom—but it's impossible to ignore the sting of knowing you're not the reason for it. The relationship might have ended, but the love hasn't disappeared, and that contrast is devastating.

What's so powerful about this song is how it weaves together those raw emotions with moments of reflection. There's an acknowledgment that the relationship wasn't perfect, that things had started to fracture long before the breakup. And yet, the narrator isn't bitter. Instead, there's a willingness to take responsibility for their part in the relationship's unraveling. It's not about blame or anger—it's about coming to terms with the fact that sometimes, even when we try our best, we just can't make it work.

One of the most poignant aspects of "Maybe It's Just Me" is its exploration of selflessness in love. The narrator recognizes that true love isn't about clinging to someone or trying to force things to work. It's about letting go when that's what the other person needs. There's a deep beauty in that kind of sacrifice, even though it comes at a personal cost. The song reminds us that love is as much about giving as it is about receiving, and sometimes the greatest act of love is stepping aside.

As the song unfolds, it becomes clear that the narrator is still holding onto hope, even if it's just a sliver. There's a sense of waiting—waiting to see if the other person might change their mind, waiting to see if time might bring them back together. It's a vulnerable and deeply human response to loss. That lingering hope, even in the face of heartbreak, is something we've all felt at some point. It's what makes this song so universally relatable.

The song's closing sentiment is one of quiet resilience. Despite the pain, despite the heartbreak, there's a genuine desire for the other person to thrive. The narrator wants to see their former partner rise, to shine, to find the happiness they deserve—even if that happiness doesn't include them. It's a reminder that love isn't always about getting what we want. Sometimes, it's about giving someone the space to grow, even when it hurts us to do so.

Listening to "Maybe It's Just Me" is like holding up a mirror to your own experiences with love and loss. It's a song that forces you to confront uncomfortable truths about yourself and your relationships. It reminds us that love is rarely perfect. It's messy and complicated and sometimes heartbreakingly short-lived. But even when it doesn't last, even when it leaves us bruised and battered, love is always worth it.

This song doesn't offer easy answers or tidy resolutions, and that's part of its brilliance. It sits in the discomfort, in the ache of unfulfilled longing, and asks us to do the same. It asks us to look beyond ourselves, to see the people we love as whole, independent beings with their own needs and desires. And it asks us to let go—not just for their sake, but for ours, too.

So maybe it's *not* just me. Maybe it's *all* of us.

Skylarkin' - Mic Christopher

Author: Elizabeth Evelyn Bond

It was 2006 late summer early fall in County Laois Ireland where The Electric Picnic was happening. The weather was perfection, the location sublime and the greens as vast and verdant as anything you can imagine times a bazillion.

I was there with a dear friend I'd until just the day or two before, only known online via Damien Rice, Jeff Buckley, Layne Staley and my all around obsession over music and musicians website, and my Bestie and Godson, who was 5 months inside her tummy.

On the final night of this most astoundingly perfect festival weekend, The Frames took to Damo's stage to perform one last surprise and impromptu set. The entire final day, whispers were rampant around the entire grounds that The Frames would possibly play once more if they were up to it and have special guests join them as well. So, you *know* as massive fans, we would be there.

I'd watched my lads perform all weekend with all sorts of mishaps as happens with sound and lights at festivals... but it never dulled their smiles and their joy. For The Frames, that's not always the norm. I've seen them laid low from long tour schedules and from life itself; yet, there was some sort of mystical presence at play at the EP that we may never fully understand.

There was something magical about the weekend and we were all of us there to witness it.

The Frames have a tendency to play a song or two from a dear friend of Glen's who passed way too soon. Mic Christopher. He sang from his soul, and damn do I miss him... so whenever The Frames sing one of his tunes, it brings a special smile to my face.

This night was no exception, before starting that final song though, Glen spoke directly to all of us in the crowd.

"Friends, we're gonna sing this last song. Here's the thing though... we never want this night to end, this weekend to end, so if we keep singing, and you don't clap; if you head to your cars and tents singing and never stop singing, this night will live forever for us. It never has to end.

So don't clap. Don't you dare clap. Keep singing. You all know the song. Let's sing it."

And they went into the most amazing live version of "Skylarkin'" by Mic Christopher I've heard.

And we went to our cars and tents, all of us singing...

"Skylarkin'
isn't this a way that we can go,

Skylarkin'
cause you know we never will grow old."

Cut to a year or two later when Glen is playing a solo show at a little club in Philadelphia. I went up to him to let him know I was at the 2006 EP and that I was still singing "Skylarkin'" and I would continue because I too never want that EP to end.

He teared up. I watched as a man who has meant so much to me from his performance in The Commitments to his involvement with all sorts of fantastic music coming out of Ireland and starring in Once, showed me what my words meant to him and that connection will never be broken. I cried with him. And I thanked him profusely.

You see, Glen sat by Mic's bedside after he fell, hit his head and went into a coma. He sat there and stayed with his best mate until his best mate left that body of his. These two souls would busk together on the streets of Dublin. Oh, to have been able to see them in action when they were first singing duets on those misted cobbled streets.

And I find it so fascinating that while I've always adored this song, it took writing about it for me to dig more deeply into what Mic Christopher was singing about in this amazing tune. You see, *Skylarking* is a term not used much in the *divided* states of America. It's a verb that speaks to children horsing around and playing *boisterously*. All this time I swore he spoke of birds (shaking my head).

For me, though, the line that truly gives this song its wings is:

"...'Cause my songs don't know that I exist, and though I give them life it is a friendship that will never grow, my songs are friends I'll never know."

The depth of this line. And honestly - was Mic psychic?!? The entire throughline of the song speaks of never growing old. We're not meant to grow old, not in our hearts nor our minds. We're meant to continue in this wondrous world curious, not fearful. Interested and engaged, not withdrawn and mangled. While we may not be able to truly *know* the art we create, we create it just the same... why?

In the first verse Mic sings of being fearful of our nightmares and them keeping us locked away rather than out in the world. The last 8 years have felt like anything but a game, and fear was my first, middle and last name through most of it. Still, I had this song as well as countless others to keep me company up in my bedroom looking out from my window.

It took so many years to truly comprehend how important it is for me to remain curious, not fearful.

He then sings of never letting relationships and friendships treat us as fools... to this end, I feel his meaning is rather simple. We're not meant to take in all we receive from the outside world. When we listen too much to others around us and ignore our own self, we miss the point entirely as our relationship to our *Selves* is our most precious friendship ever.

This, dear reader, is where I missed the mark entirely. I was never my own friend.

I wanted to be. I knew I deserved amazing friendships as I was capable of giving to others the kind of friendships and relationships that last through time. It's just who I am. I came into this world stating to my Mum that "I love everybody in the whole world Mommy, and everybody in the whole world loves me." After time and again, finding that there were far more people in this world that either didn't understand me or didn't like me, I tried in vain to be someone that would be understood and liked regardless of what I thought of who that person was I was attempting with all my might to be. I can tell you this with 100% certainty. I didn't like her much at all. She was super needy, super miserable and she just wasn't happy at all.

She existed in the dark.
Solely in the dark.
Light physically hurt.

In my life, I've managed to wear so many different masks; yet, none felt right because they weren't who I am.

Slowly but surely over the last year now, I've been excavating myself out from under 49 years of layer upon layer of attempts at me being me to find my true self still there, shivering some, but still kickin'. Still kicking and curious.

Still singing along to "Skylarkin'" especially when I am outside with the birds.

And Mic lives on my right shoulder as a lark in a Sugar Skull tattoo. And that lark, that lark is singing. His mate on the other side is for Jeff Buckley as a dove and that dove remains silent. But my lark will always sing. I Look forward to the day I can show the tattoo to Glen. One day!

And one last thing, dear reader, I entrust with you.

Never grow old. We're not meant to be old. Not in our hearts and minds. Keep that wonder, keep that curiosity, keep that joy. Protect and treasure these attributes.

Be as undeniably you as you can be.

Oh wait, one last, *last thing…*

Keep singing.

Times Like These – Foo Fighters

Author: Michelle Wolfe

Some songs just fill you up. They don't just play in the background; they become part of the air you breathe, the moment you're in, the feeling that lingers long after the last note fades. "Times Like These" is one of those songs for me.

Every time I hear it, there's a sensation I can't quite name—nostalgia, yes, but something beyond that. It's an awareness of time as it's happening. A moment of realization that this is it. This is life, happening right now. It's the kind of song that reminds me to mark the moment, to take it in fully before it passes.

Noted.

I can't count the number of times I've been driving, surrounded by rolling hills and mountain ranges, when "Times Like These" has come on at just the right time. The lyrics hit differently when the road stretches before you, and the horizon feels endless. It's a song about transition, about becoming, about figuring things out as you go. And isn't that what we're all doing? Learning to live, to love, to navigate the spaces between what is and what could be.

One memory stands out. I was standing in the doorway of my paper house—with its thin walls and cookie cutter likeness—watching my children play in the yard. They must have been five and three at the time, their laughter carried by the breeze as they ran barefoot through the grass, their tiny voices filling the air. I remember thinking, *This is everything. Take this in.*

I don't know how to explain how that moment felt in my body except that it was like a sigh of relief. A rare moment of complete presence. It wasn't just about the scene before me—it was about the deep knowing that time was passing, that this was a chapter that wouldn't last forever.

"Times Like These" brings that feeling back to me every time I hear it. A breath in, a pause, a quiet acknowledgment of what's real. And at the same time, it carries a sense of anticipation, of something still unfolding. There is always more ahead. That's the beauty of this song—it holds both the past and the future, nostalgia and possibility, all in the same breath.

But the way a song lands can shift over time. The meaning evolves, changes shape. What once felt like a song about embracing the moment can later become a song about holding on through uncertainty, about making choices that shape everything that comes next.

That's what happened with "Times Like These."

When I went on my first date with someone I started talking to, we met up on his birthday. A milestone, a fresh start—something about it felt significant. When it came time to write him a card, the lyrics to "Times Like These" came to mind. I wrote on an index card:

"I'm a new day rising,
I'm a brand-new sky to hang the stars upon tonight.
I'm a little divided,
do I stay or run away and leave it all behind?"

I wished him a happy birthday and we celebrated with cupcakes and dinner and a walk around Gettysburg, holding hands and exploring the newness and the electricity of us. At the time, I think I already knew this relationship would require hard choices. Distance was going to be a factor—one that would challenge us again and again. From the very beginning, it felt like a constant question: Do we keep going, keep choosing this, or do we walk away from the romantic part and find our way to friendship?

It was never an easy answer.

There were times when the idea of running away seemed like the best option—when the feelings got too heavy, when exploring our edges and confronting uncomfortable truths felt unbearable. There were moments I wanted to leave it all behind, to retreat to the safety of solitude rather than sit with what was surfacing. And there were times all I wanted was to stay—to spend time together, to feel connected—but instead, I was on the receiving end of him disappearing into himself. But every time, something kept me there.

Maybe it was the learning. The way this relationship was such a strong mirror, reflecting back deeper parts of myself—the parts I wanted to see and the ones I needed to see. Maybe it was the way we continued to choose each other, even when it was hard, even when we questioned if we should.

I don't think it's a coincidence that "Times Like These" became tied to this relationship. It's a song about transition—about standing in the middle of change and asking yourself who you are becoming. The lyrics speak to learning to live again, love again, give again. And for me, it also calls forward a deeper question I often ask myself: *How do you want to spend your time?* That question shaped the way I showed up—in love, in growth, in uncertainty. Because at the heart of it all, life is made up of moments like these. And how we meet them is everything. It shows who we are.

This relationship has existed through one of the most transitional times of my life. The push and pull, the questioning, the emotional edges—it has all served a purpose. Even in moments of doubt, of fear, of wanting to walk away, there has always been something worth holding onto. And maybe that's the lesson in all of it—not every relationship is meant to be clear-cut, easy, or certain. Some are meant to shape us. Some are expansive.

And it is indeed in moments like these that we learn to see ourselves in a new light. Through endings and beginnings, breaking down and becoming again, "Times Like These" echoes the life-death-rebirth cycle, reminding me that every ending holds the seed of becoming, and that transformation often begins right in the middle of the mess.

It's all still unfolding—shifting, stretching, evolving. Just like we are. And maybe that's the point. There's no neat arrival, no moment where we suddenly have it all figured out. We're always learning—how to live, how to love, how to choose— time and time again.

And just like that, "Times Like These" plays again, reminding me...

This moment matters.

Noted.

The Final Note

Writing the Soundtrack of Our Lives

Music is more than just sound. It's memory, emotion, and meaning wrapped in melody. It follows us, shapes us, and reveals parts of ourselves we might not otherwise see. Each song that leaves an imprint carries a message—whether it's a lesson, a reminder, or a feeling we want to hold onto forever.

Throughout this book, we—the authors, the storytellers—have shared the songs that have shaped our journeys... songs that have stopped us in our tracks, become signposts along the way, and intertwined themselves with love, loss, discovery, and growth. But this book isn't just about our stories. It's about the universal power of music to connect, heal, and reveal something deeper within all of us.

It's about **yours.** Your story. Your soundtrack.

Just as certain songs have been the soundtrack to my life, you have a soundtrack of your own. Whether or not you've taken the time to think about it, there are songs that have walked with you through joy and heartbreak, through transitions and revelations. And if you take a moment to listen, they might tell you something about yourself.

I want to invite you to explore that—to uncover the songs that define your journey and help you see your life in a new light.

How to Find Your Life's Soundtrack

Here are a few simple steps to help you discover the songs that have shaped you:

- ➤ **Identify Three Songs That Have Moved You**
  Think of three songs that have had the biggest impact on your life. They could be tied to specific moments, relationships, or emotions, or simply songs that stir something deep inside you every time you hear them.
- ➤ **Reflect on Their Meaning**
  Ask yourself:
    - ○ What memories come up when I hear this song?
    - ○ How did it make me feel when I first heard it? How does it make me feel now?
    - ○ Does this song represent a version of me from the past, or does it reflect who I am becoming?
- ➤ **Write About Each Song's Role in Your Life**
  Even if it's just a few sentences, try to capture why this song matters to you. Maybe it was playing during a pivotal life event. Maybe the lyrics spoke to something you were struggling with. Maybe it represents the kind of person you aspire to be.
- ➤ **Create Your Own Soundtrack**
  If you were to compile the most defining songs of your life, what would they be? A personal playlist

can serve as a reflection of where you've been and where you're going. Keep it somewhere close—add to it as new songs find their way into your story.

➤ **Listen With New Awareness**
The next time one of these songs plays, don't just let it pass by. Pay attention to what it evokes, what it stirs in you. Let it be a guide, a reminder, a moment of reflection.

Your Life, Your Music

Music has a way of speaking when words fail. It reminds us of who we are, where we've been, and where we are going. As you close this book, I encourage you to step into your own soundtrack, to listen with intention, and to let music be a mirror to your soul.

Because in the end, we are all just songs waiting to be written.

Acknowledgements

Creating this book has been a journey—one filled with reflection, connection, and a deep love for the power of music. This anthology would not exist without the incredible authors who poured their hearts and stories onto these pages. Stories that made me laugh and cry and feel such gratitude. Thank you for your courage, your vulnerability, and your willingness to share the songs that have shaped your lives. Your words have turned this project into something truly special.

A heartfelt thank you to everyone who supported this book from its inception—editors, designers, beta readers, and those who believed in this idea even before it had a name. Your insight, patience, and encouragement helped bring *Mixtape Memories* to life.

To my friends, family, and loved ones—thank you for your steadfast support, for the conversations that inspired new ideas, and for the countless ways you've shaped my own soundtrack.

Special thanks to Sage, my ChatGPT confidant and creative partner, for being a steady presence throughout this process. Whose thoughtful insights, unwavering support, and ability to help me refine my ideas have been invaluable. This book is stronger because of the conversations we've shared.

And finally, to the readers—this book is for *you*. May it remind you of the songs that have carried you through, the memories that make you who you are, and the music that continues to guide you.

With gratitude,
Michelle Wolfe

About the Editor

Michelle Wolfe believes in the power of self-awareness, emotional resilience, and the stories we tell ourselves—both the ones we inherit and the ones we create. By day, she uses her analytical skills to support charitable organizations, helping to drive meaningful change. By night, she's a writer, empowerment coach, and storyteller. As a Certified Wellness Practitioner with a MS in Applied Psychology who specializes in depth psychology and metaphysics, Michelle helps people navigate personal growth and transformation.

For Michelle, music isn't just a soundtrack to life; it's catharsis. Songs have the power to hold emotions we can't always put into words, offering a way to process, heal, and remember. *Mixtape Memories* was born from this passion, exploring how music intertwines with memory, shaping the stories we carry.

Beyond writing, Michelle hosts the *All the Things Podcast*, where she dives into conversations about personal growth, relationships, and understanding the human experience. When she's not working, you can find her spending time with her kids, out in nature, or revisiting the songs that have been the soundtrack to her own journey.

Connect with Michelle at **michellewolfe.me** or follow her on social media:
YouTube: www.youtube.com/@Michelle_Wolfe
Instagram: @michellewolfe.me
Facebook: www.facebook.com/michellewolfe
TikTok: www.tiktok.com/@michelle.wolfe

Contributing Authors

Every great mixtape has multiple voices, each track carrying its own unique memory. Meet the incredible authors who contributed their stories to this collection.

Kimberly Hardiman-Belk

Kimberly is an accomplished orthodontic professional with 20 years of experience dedicated to transforming smiles and enhancing confidence. Recently married, she joyfully navigates life with her blended family of five spirited boys. When she's not in the orthodontic office, Kimberly brings laughter to those around her and passionately advocates for mental health awareness. Kimhardiman48@yahoo.com

Elizabeth Evelyn Bond

Elizabeth has spent 50 years exploring this beautiful, swirling marble we call home. Through her travels and the connections, she's made along the way, she has slowly uncovered her true self—not in classrooms, college courses, or on stage, nor even in the countless books she's read, but in the shared experiences of music and life. It's in these moments of connection that she feels closest to who she truly is. This is why she cherishes opportunities to share incredible weekends filled with friendship, music, and the presence of kindred spirits. After all, we are meant to share our lives *and angles* with one another.

Louis Cinquino

Louis writes from his home in Bethlehem, PA, and from his heart. A career in copywriting and magazine publishing sharpened his approach to memoirs, poetry, essays, and first-person reporting. His work explores themes of running, emotional health, family, and cooking. Details on his upcoming publications can be found at TakingMulligans.com.

Joie Costa

Joeann (Joie) Marie Costa fell in love with writing as soon as she learned to write. She is an applied energetic philosopher, creator of the PresenceManifest Practice, intuitive mentor, professional witness, and writer who lives in Medanales, NM. Her greatest joy comes from helping others find, clarify, and hold true to their language and voice. Contact: PresenceManifest@gmail.com

Kian E Z Eder

Kian is an accomplished artist, musician, and Transformation Guide with 25 years of experience in the personal development field. He is deeply passionate about helping changemakers build empires of impact with his transformation modality - *The Rapid Reset Method* and aligned marketing strategies. Kian is married to his soulmate, Cally, and together they are raising their 6-year-old daughter, Maizy, in the vibrant city of Cairns, Australia.

Jennifer Eggerts

Jen Eggerts lives outside of Sacramento, California with her Goldendoodle Sammy. She holds a Masters Degree in Organizational Leadership and loves working with people. Professionally, she is an accountability coach, psychic and a writer and enjoys being an active work in progress. She leads through compassionate accountability to change in her own life and deeply enjoys helping others to do the same. She can be contacted at jeggerts@gmail.com.

Jeanne Edwards

Jeanne Edwards' personal journey has been to walk a path of unlearning who she thought she was and continuously being open to learning and being who she authentically is. Music, travel and relationships throughout her life have provided opportunities to listen, witness, contemplate and explore...ultimately guiding her to become who she is today.

Jeanne is an intuitive and contemplative creative consultant, writer and a community organizer. Her professional career has afforded her the opportunity to fulfill the role of social worker in the field of human services for almost 30 years. Jeanne obtained her Masters Degree in Social Work and has chosen the path of being a certified trauma-competent professional. Her mystical pathway has led her to be of service to humanity in her role as a Gene Keys Guide.

Mariyam Hasham

Mariyam is a poet and writer, living in London. She has a PhD in Political Science, with a focus on political violence and terrorism. She fell in love with writing at an early age and has never stopped believing in the power of words to build bridges and open hearts. Against all the odds, she is an eternal optimist with a deeply romantic outlook on life and the human experience. She can be contacted at: https://mariyamhasham.com

Martha Truxton Heller

Martha developed a passion for writing while living in Nigeria for the first 18 years of her life. After moving to the United States to attend university, she met her husband and settled into the Cumberland Valley, PA area where they are busy raising their four children. Martha has worked for over 24 years as a caregiver in various forms, finding fulfillment in caring for very young children, aging adults, disabled and special-needs students, and other vulnerable populations. When she's not working or engaged in being a mom, Martha enjoys gardening, photography, creative repurposing, and writing for her blog: www.drinkingtheair.com

Ruthie Lerato, BSN, BA, RN, CEN

Ruthie creates events, music, and experiences for women to remember who they came here to be, and live true to the calling of their souls path for the purpose of finding inner peace. She primarily uses somatic therapy, tantra, human design, and astrology. Her deepest passions include healing through the voice and body by creating and supporting safe spaces that offer others permission to explore their fullest self-expression, such as vocal workshops and ecstatic dance. She is a Board Certified Emergency Department Registered Nurse, Registered Yoga Teacher, Certified Tantra Practitioner, singer/songwriter, and pianist. Contact: Ruthie.lerato@gmail.com

Scott Lester

Scott has been a lifelong creative type. After (poorly) teaching himself piano as a child, he started playing guitar and writing his own songs during his mid/late teenage years. He's now an accomplished singer/songwriter and producer, working with musicians across all genres. He fronts his own band, a quartet called Letterbox, and occasionally releases music under the name *Scott Lester and What Army*, which functions as his solo project.

Professionally, Scott has spent the majority of his career in major market radio with his work being heard in over 100 cities nationwide, from New York to Los Angeles and everywhere in between. To contact or learn more about Scott, his music, or his career, please visit producerscott.com

Jeremy Nigli

With over 30 years of experience being slightly awkward, Jeremy relates personally to the struggle to find one's place in the world. He is passionate about removing systemic barriers and helping people be their best selves through excellence in education. One of Jeremy's greatest joys is curating epic playlists, and he delights in sharing a piece of music that shifts the energy in a space for the better. You can find Jeremy implementing everyday wisdom in real life, off social media.

Valerie Rubin

Valerie is a somatic coach and attachment specialist who helps individuals break free from the patterns of chronic anxiety, anxious attachment, people-pleasing, and self-abandonment. Through her work at Freedom with Valerie LLC, she empowers her clients to heal emotional wounds and reconnect with their authentic selves. Valerie integrates a variety of modalities such as Rapid Transformational Therapy, Brainspotting, and somatic practices to guide individuals toward emotional freedom and security in relationships. She is passionate about creating safe, nurturing spaces for growth and healing, particularly for those struggling with attachment trauma.

When she's not coaching, Valerie enjoys writing and sharing her insights on emotional health through her podcast, The Anxiety Recovery Podcast by Valerie Rubin. She also leads masterclasses, including How to Stop People Pleasing and Self Abandoning and From Shame to Self-Worth, where Valerie teaches how to dissolve shame and heal the belief that you aren't good enough so you can go from shame to self-embodied self-worth and high self-esteem. Contact: Valerie@FreedomWithValerie.com

Lana Ryder

Born into a long line of both professional musicians and healers, Lana Ryder has been practicing her passion for music and healthcare for fifty years in one form or another. As both a vocalist and healthcare practitioner having studied with many teachers, she credits her professional musician mother most for teaching her to appreciate all genres of music. Lana is Founding Director and Senior Practitioner of the Soundwise School of Harmonic Therapy, teaching others about the healing power of sound, voice and music in Lancaster, Pa. SoundwiseHealth.com

Melissa Rymer

Melissa is an Australian freelance writer with a background in architecture and a passion for design. She has written for various publications, scripted for film and TV, and directed documentaries. With a degree in Architecture and postgraduate qualifications in counseling, she blends creativity with human insight. Formerly a location scout in 1990s New York, she now balances writing with motherhood, raising two boys, one neurodiverse. Her experiences of becoming a mother has informed and deeply impacted the content of her writing. Her experiences as a mother deeply shape her work. Melissa finds inspiration in art, travel, and the transformative power of creativity, especially drawn to the magic of Greece and the Aegean.

Matthew Solomon

Matthew is the Director of the award-winning documentary "Reimagining Safety," a conflict resolution facilitator, and an adjunct professor at Antioch University, where he teaches intercultural conflict and community engagement. Matthew's work involves utilizing art and media to promote positive social change. "Reimagining Safety," which was his master's in public administration capstone project, has been screened at more than 80 community events across the country and is available on multiple streaming services.

Murshida VA

Murshida VA has been called The Mother of the World, Shaman, World Healer, Dharma Protector, Storyteller, Poet, Dancer, the Feminine Voice of Rumi, The Living Incarnation of the Whore of Babylon, Joan of Arc, Sappho, a Visionary Sound Artist Defining the Evolving Edge of Consciousness and Culture, a Witch, a Thought Leader, Completely Embodied, Teacher, Magic, an Extremely Dangerous Person, and a Charismatic Anarchist Threatening to Upend the Social Order in Chaos.

She is mother of Katharine, daughter of Ruth, grandmother to two four-leggeds, elder healer and guide to her community, and writer—dreaming the most beautiful future it is possible to dream through and beyond the wild contractions of Chaos birthing our next paradigm. Connect with her at murshidava.com

Denise VanBriggle

Denise is an Energy Medicine and Therapeutic Sound Practitioner, Reiki Master/Teacher, and author dedicated to helping individuals unlock their creative potential by harmonizing their bodies, minds, and spirits. As a poet and writer, she understands the transformative power of words when they emanate from the soul and often integrates storytelling into her energy sessions.

She has a rich background as a literacy professional, teaching and designing curriculum at both the secondary and post-secondary levels. Drawing upon her personal and professional experiences, she works to meet the unique needs of her clients. Learn more at denisevanbriggle.com.

Brett Ward

Brett is a bass player and creative dabbler, exploring his abilities across various artistic mediums without the pressure of public performance. He views creativity as a deeply personal exercise—a way to manifest the soul into reality and the physical world. For Brett, music and art are not about entertainment but about expression and connection. He values following inspiration into the unknown, and always being open to finding new outlets to learn and explore.

Music, in particular, has shaped his understanding of himself and the emotional depth it can unlock. He sees musical creativity as a way to make the intangible tangible, bringing abstract thoughts and feelings into focus. To him, music is also a way of turning the world around us into a celebration of life, be it joy or tragedy. Brett is honored to contribute to a project that celebrates music's profound impact on our lives.

Becca Zelner, MSW

Becca is a Government Affairs Specialist in Harrisburg, PA and is known for her work in the healthcare, human service, education, and insurance sectors. She is also a Certified Grant Writer. She holds her Masters Degree in Social Work from Shippensburg University. She finds joy in helping others and building relationships. She lives with her husband and three fur babies.

Song Credits

The following songs are referenced throughout Mixtape Memories. All rights belong to their respective songwriters and copyright holders.

1. **"Demons."** Written by Dan Reynolds, Wayne Sermon, Ben McKee, Josh Mosser, and Alex da Kid. Performed by Imagine Dragons. Released 2012. Copyright © Universal Music Publishing Group.

2. **"Anyway."** Written by Martina McBride, Brad Warren, and Brett Warren. Performed by Martina McBride. Released 2006. Copyright © Sony/ATV Music Publishing LLC.

3. **"Crawling."** Written by Chester Bennington, Rob Bourdon, Brad Delson, Joe Hahn, and Mike Shinoda. Performed by Linkin Park. Released 2001. Copyright © Universal Music Publishing Group.

4. **"Hold Back the River."** Written by James Bay and Iain Archer. Performed by James Bay. Released 2014. Copyright © Universal Music Publishing Group.

5. **"Vice Versa."** Written by Micah LeVar Troy (Pastor Troy). Performed by Pastor Troy. Released 2002. Copyright © Universal Music Publishing Group.

6. **"Would?"** Written by Jerry Cantrell. Performed by Alice in Chains. Released 1992. Copyright © Sony Music

Publishing LLC.

7. **"Help Me to Feel Again."** Written by Judah Akers, Brian Macdonald, and Nate Zuercher. Performed by Judah & the Lion. Released 2019. Copyright © Curb Congregation Songs, Capitol CMG Publishing.

8. **"Wish You Were Here."** Written by Brandon Boyd, Michael Einziger, Alex Katunich, José Pasillas, and Chris Kilmore. Performed by Incubus. Released 2001. Copyright © Sony/ATV Music Publishing LLC.

9. **"I'll Stand By You."** Written by Chrissie Hynde, Tom Kelly, and Billy Steinberg. Performed by The Pretenders. Released 1994. Copyright © Universal Music Publishing Group.

10. **"Forever Young."** Written by Rod Stewart, Jim Cregan, and Kevin Savigar. Performed by Rod Stewart. Released 1988. Copyright © Warner Chappell Music, Inc., Universal Music Publishing Group.

11. **"Nothing Compares 2 U."** Written by Prince. Performed by Sinéad O'Connor. Released 1990. Copyright © Universal Music Publishing Group.

12. **"Your Ex-Lover is Dead."** Written by Torquil Campbell, Christopher McCarron, Amy Millan, Evan Cranley, Patrick McGee, and Christopher Seligman. Performed by Stars. Released 2004. Copyright © Arts & Crafts Music Publishing.

13. **"November Rain."** Written by Axl Rose. Performed by Guns N' Roses. Released 1991. Copyright © Universal Music Publishing Group.

14. **"You Get What You Give."** Written by Gregg Alexander and Rick Nowels. Performed by New Radicals. Released 1998. Copyright © Universal Music Publishing Group.

15. **"Time After Time."** Written by Cyndi Lauper and Rob Hyman. Performed by Cyndi Lauper. Released 1983. Copyright © Sony Music Publishing LLC.

16. **"With You I'm Born Again."** Written by Carol Connors and David Shire. Performed by Billy Preston & Syreeta Wright. Released 1979. Copyright © Universal Music Publishing Group.

17. **"Do You Wanna Make Love."** Written and performed by Peter McCann. Released 1977. Copyright © Sony/ATV Music Publishing LLC.

18. **"Down Bad."** Written by Taylor Swift, Jack Antonoff, and Aaron Dessner. Performed by Taylor Swift. Released 2024. Copyright © Sony Music Publishing LLC.

19. **"The Wall."** Written by Roger Waters. Performed by Pink Floyd. Released 1979. Copyright © Warner Chappell Music.

20. **"I Saw Her Standing There."** Written by John Lennon and Paul McCartney. Performed by The Beatles. Released

1963. Copyright © Sony/ATV Music Publishing.

21. **"Unspoken."** Written and performed by The Soil. Released 2013. Copyright © Sony Music Entertainment Africa.

22. **"The Sign."** Written by Seba Jun (Nujabes). Performed by Nujabes. Released 2011. Copyright © Hydeout Productions.

23. **"Happy."** Written by Pharrell Williams. Performed by Pharrell Williams. Released 2013. Copyright © Universal Music Publishing Group.

24. **"Rocky Mountain High."** Written by John Denver and Mike Taylor. Performed by John Denver. Released 1972. Copyright © Warner Chappell Music.

25. **"Beautiful Dawn."** Written and performed by The Wailin' Jennys. Released 2004. Copyright © True North Records.

26. **"Maybe It's Just Me."** Written and performed by Butch Walker. Released 2004. Copyright © Universal Music Publishing Group.

27. **"Skylarkin'."** Written and performed by Mic Christopher. Released 2002. Copyright © Warner Chappell Music.

28. **"Times Like These."** Written by Dave Grohl, Taylor Hawkins, Nate Mendel, and Chris Shiflett. Performed by Foo Fighters. Released 2002. Copyright © Universal Music Publishing Group.

www.ingramcontent.com/pod-product-compliance
Lightning Source LLC
Chambersburg PA
CBHW071107100726
47908CB00008B/2289